of Jesus in the 24 chapters of the Gospel of Luke. The \[...]
on the 25th day uses John 1 to underscore the mystery and marvel of the incarnation of the Son of God. The Process, Prayer, and Promise section at the end of each day effectively encourages the user to personally apply the principles developed on each of the 25 days. This is a great tool to prepare us for the coming of the Lord into space-time history and into our lives." —**Kenneth Boa**, President, Reflections Ministries, Omnibus Media, and Trinity House Publishers

"We are invited to know the love of Jesus for us on every page of this warm, engaging, and relatable devotional filled with life-giving gospel truths and promises. Read these as daily encouragement for your own heart or with your teenagers at Christmas and process together how Jesus matters for each of us every day." —**Susan Crenshaw**, First Lady, Young Life

"God's Word teaches us that 'as a man thinks in his heart, so is he.' As Christmas approaches year after year, we easily find ourselves far from the things on which we need to be focused. Using Anna's and Katy's Christmas devotional is a great aid in adjusting that focus. *Christmas Matters* is a short, to-the-point, and engaging read. It is a tremendous resource to add to your daily time with God for the 25 days leading up to Christmas." —**Randy Pope**, Founding Pastor, Perimeter Church; President, Life on Life Ministries

"A jewel of a devotional book that reaches past the clutter and busyness of Christmas and speaks to the heart of the holiday. I plan to use it every December." —**Emily Carpenter**, best-selling author of *Burying the Honeysuckle Girls*

"*Christmas Matters* is a gift to the reader—a fresh perspective on a story we know so well but sometimes forget how life-changing it is. Using scriptural insights, personal anecdotes, and godly wisdom, Anna and Katy take us on a journey from the anticipation of the Messiah to the empty tomb in a way that is sure to leave us changed." —**Jennifer Phillips**, author of *Hope When It's Hard* and coauthor of *Unhitching from the Crazy Train*

"The Christmas season is one of the most anticipated and memory-filled seasons of the year. It can also be the most exhausting and stressful season of the year. Anna Nash and Katy Shelton now offer us a remedy for the stress and exhaustion of our favorite season through their devotional book, *Christmas Matters*. This powerfully inspirational book helps us focus our thoughts on Christ, the only part of the Christmas season that truly matters. With attention-grabbing stories, focused biblical truth, and daily rituals of reflection, *Christmas Matters* is the perfect companion for the Christmas season. I highly recommend!" —**Sara W. Berry**, coauthor of the best-selling book *Tap Code* and the award-winning book *The Summer of 1969*; author of *Gathering Stones*

"*Christmas Matters* is a work from a fresh perspective. This Advent daily devotional is for anyone who hopes to connect with the true spirit of Christmas amid the seasonal chaos of shopping, wrapping gifts, sending cards, cooking, and visiting relatives. Each day's offering leads the reader along a path that not only culminates in "Triumph" but also provides thought-provoking reflections that help us to see the face of Christ in the crush of the shopping mall crowd and helps us to hear the voice of Jesus over the din of the same old Christmas carols we've been listening to since Halloween. Seeing and hearing Christ in this season is important because the birth of Jesus does make a difference every day—if we "Anticipate," "Receive," "Hope," and "Proclaim," as these daily readings show us. Nash and Shelton have opened the door to the relational character of Christ with us, not to tell us who He is in theological terms but to encourage us to discover who we are with Him as Christ Child, Friend, Teacher, Healer, and Redeemer. Meeting Christ through Luke's eyes and hearing Him in the physician's eloquent voice through his Gospel, as pondered by the writers, is an opportunity to view Christmas from an intimate perspective and an invitation that will reward us for Christmases to come if we accept it." —**Betsy Iler**, Editor, *Lake* magazine

Christmas Matters

HOW THE BIRTH OF JESUS MAKES
A DIFFERENCE EVERY DAY

A CHRISTMAS DEVOTIONAL

ANNA NASH *and* KATY SHELTON

BIRMINGHAM, ALABAMA

Christmas Matters

Iron Stream
An imprint of Iron Stream Media
100 Missionary Ridge
Birmingham, AL 35242
IronStreamMedia.com

Library of Congress Control Number: 2021940361

A previous edition of this book was produced and sold by SCWC Books, a division of the Southern Christian Writers Conference.
www.southernchristianwriters.com

Scripture quotations are from the ESV® Bible (The Holy Bible, English Standard Version®), copyright © 2001 by Crossway, a publishing ministry of Good News Publishers. Used by permission. All rights reserved.

ISBN: 978-1-56309-544-3 paperback
ISBN: 978-1-56309-545-0 ebook

1 2 3 4 5—25 24 23 22 21
Printed in the United States of America

To Jane and Anne, our mamas,
for teaching us from the beginning that Jesus matters every day

Contents

Note to the Reader

We go way back. I'm not talking about a few years of way back, I'm talking about a lifetime of way back. Our mothers connected soon after we were born, and in fact at the time, Anna's mother led Katy's mother to Jesus. As a result, our friendship began. We were childhood friends, high school friends, and college roommates.

After marrying and raising our children in different states, we reconnected, but this time in a different way. We found ourselves at that empty-nest, middle stage in life, and we both wanted more. We did not want to settle down or retire; we wanted to start over, to begin anew. We wanted to make a difference.

Anna founded a ministry called Beacon People, centered on helping people understand how to intentionally live a more purposeful and meaningful life and helping them align their lives with whom God created them to be. Katy discovered a new passion for writing and editing, and she was filled with more ideas and projects than she had time to explore.

That's when our lives once again merged. Anna needed an editor for Beacon People. Katy needed to hone her new writing and editing skills. And so the collaboration began. In 2016, a beautiful and meaningful working partnership was born.

Fast-forward a few years to a new idea for a project: a book intended to help place focus on Jesus—His birth, His life, His death, and His resurrection—at Christmastime. Anna accepted Katy's challenge, and they began writing. The book became a daily journey through the twenty-four chapters of the Gospel of

Luke to coincide with the twenty-four days in December leading to Christmas. It ends on Christmas Day with a celebration of Jesus's life based on the first chapter of John. In writing this book, our greatest desire is simply to help others focus on our Savior, the Messiah, during Christmas and beyond.

We welcome you to join us on an exciting and inspiring journey as we allow Jesus to make a difference in our lives today and every day.

Anna and Katy

How to Use This Book

Welcome and thank you for joining us on a journey through the twenty-four chapters of the Gospel of Luke. Beginning on December 1, we will read a chapter a day from Luke that coincides with the chapter in *Christmas Matters*, taking us through the twenty-four days in December leading to Christmas. Together we will celebrate Jesus's birth, life, death, and resurrection during this sacred season. We are so honored to celebrate the Messiah with you.

Time and again in the book of Luke we find Jesus touching the lives of individuals in the most gracious of ways. Drawing people in with His lovingkindness, He then captured their hearts and called them to a more meaningful life. He didn't heal them for healing alone. He didn't change their perspective for peace alone. He didn't forgive their sins for relief alone. Jesus intended so much more. He thought and acted beyond the moment of personal interaction. Once a person was touched by Him, He often gave them a directive that involved "now go and do." In today's culture, this is known as a "call to action." The profound impact of Jesus's unconditional love and grace generated a desire not only to believe but also to go and live a purposeful life for Him.

Christmas Matters will bring inspiration and encouragement as you explore the stories of Jesus in Luke's narrative, and it will also extend a personal invitation to take the truths discovered and apply them to your life. Our book is intended as a guide or supplement to Luke's account of Jesus's time on earth. It in no way covers every detail of the Gospel of Luke, but rather it is intended to focus on significant truths taken from each chapter. We strongly encourage everyone to read the entire chapter of Luke upon which each chapter in the book is based as you journey with us toward Christmas. This will provide important context and a clear picture of what we all need to know about the Savior's time on earth.

In each reading you will find:

- **An overview verse** from the chapter in Luke.
- **A reflective reading** to learn more about and draw encouragement from Jesus's life.
- **A process** including thoughts or questions to help you apply what you've read.
- **A prayer** that provides an opportunity to move into conversation with God, talking and listening to Him. These prayers simply open the door for you to begin a meaningful dialogue with Him.
- **A promise** from the Bible reminding you of the freedom and reward found in the hope that Jesus offers.

As you read through the book of Luke during the Christmas season, you, too, have the opportunity to encounter Jesus in a personal way. If you choose to believe and pursue a relationship with Him, He will change your overall life perspective and offer you unexplainable joy. It is our desire to guide you into an all-encompassing and life-changing journey that is available when you respond by accepting His truths. These truths will fill your heart as you see Him not just as a historical figure or distant God but trust Him more intimately as a Savior and friend. This Christmas, let's ask God to provide new ways to help us celebrate Him as we look at the life of Jesus through the eyes of Luke.

Introduction

Tiny fingers pulled open a cardboard door labeled "December 1." Behind the door lay a Christmas-shaped piece of chocolate. It might have been a lamb or a manger or an angel or a tree, but each of the doors held a great revelation for my sister and me. Filled with anticipation, we awoke every morning of December, excited to find out what lay behind the next door.

In the Bible, the story of Christmas begins with an invitation. Luke invites us into a different time and a different place, one full of fascinating people and stories. These people were anticipating a special event. They were waiting for their Savior, who was to appear in the form of a little baby named Jesus.

My sister and I had no idea that this anticipation was called Advent. With our simple faith, we knew the calendar would be waiting for us with another treat each morning of December. We thought it was about a piece of candy, but our mother knew it was a way to point us to Jesus. Similarly, we have the opportunity to get to know the people in the book of Luke as we read each chapter, connect with God, and experience the powerful life of Jesus.

Luke explains his motivation for writing this book in the first few verses of chapter one: "to write an orderly account for you . . . that you may have certainty concerning the things you have been taught" (Luke 1:3–4).

Most people think the word *Advent* means "waiting or anticipation," but this isn't the case. *Advent* means "arrival." Jesus would arrive on earth to bring hope to all humanity. As we move into our journey to experience Him, may we focus on the beautiful gift of His birth. Advent will offer an astounding and moving experience as we prayerfully set our hearts and minds on Jesus and worship Him for who He is and what He offers.

Each of the twenty-four chapters of Luke will take us through the story of Jesus's life and the hope that He brings. Over the next month, we invite you to join us as we open one door of Luke at a time. Behind each door, we will find truth that will stir us within as we count down the days leading to Christmas. Every chapter in Luke will reveal amazing revelations that will piece together the beautiful story of God's Son and the gifts He brings.

This twenty-five-day journey will remind us of the hope that lies in the true story of Christmas. It will walk us through the Advent season, one beautiful revelation at a time. The journey will provide certainty concerning the life of Jesus as we draw near to Him. Each chapter in the book of Luke will offer us a chance to be reminded of the joyous birth of our Savior. Welcome to the season of evergreen trees, familiar carols, and sparkling lights. These are all hints of what is to come. This December, may we have an enlightening Advent journey like never before as we witness the arrival of the true light of the world.

Luke 1—Anticipate

You will have joy and gladness, and many will rejoice at his birth.

—Luke 1:14

As we open the pages of Luke 1, we feel the first touch of Christmas in the air.

One of my favorite Christmas movies, *Family Man*, has a scene in which a young married couple wakes on the morning of their wedding anniversary. While the husband showers, shaves, and dresses for work, his wife jumps from the bed and grabs the anniversary gift she picked out for him. She is bursting with excitement, hardly able to wait for him to open the present. When he returns to the room, she bounces on the bed, shakes the wrapped gift, and beams from ear to ear. "Open it!" she begs, placing the gift in front of him and beating its top like a drum.

Every year as the pile of presents beneath the Christmas tree grows, we laugh and try to guess what lies inside the beautifully wrapped boxes. "Please, just give me a hint," we say to one another. I remember as a small child whispering in the ear of my mom or dad or sister, revealing the secret of certain presents and always making them promise not to tell.

What is so special about gift giving? Anticipation. When you find the ideal gift for someone you love, it's difficult to wait for December 25 to arrive. You give hints and clues. Sometimes the recipient will shake and rattle the package trying to guess what lies beneath the shiny paper and bows. Some people don't mind opening gifts early, but others are opposed, and here's why. Much of the excitement involves anticipation, and as we wait, that excitement builds.

Anticipation of the Messiah's birth began from words spoken hundreds of years before by the prophet Isaiah. An inkling. A hint. A sort of whisper spoken in the darkness. We're told that John the Baptist would be the voice that followed the promise of the prophets. "Prepare the way of the LORD!" Isaiah prophesied in chapter 40 verse 3.

The world lived in darkness and spiritual drought for approximately four hundred years. God seemed silent for a long time. But His children (the children of Israel) were holding tightly to His promise. They were not without hope because, you see, the prophets had assured them countless times before in the Old Testament that there would be a Savior, a Rescuer, and a Redeemer. To say they were anticipating this gift is an understatement! Anticipation had given birth to a longing, a full expectation, even an impatience for what was to come. This preceded the baby Jesus's birth in Bethlehem as prophesied so many years before. The manger held the King of Kings. Yes, those present were astounded, but the joy of the heavenly Father was indescribable, I'm sure.

Where do we fit into the story? What are we hoping or longing for? Often we get overwhelmed or confused by the idea of God and His Son, Jesus. Maybe the story seems overfamiliar, or maybe it feels unrelatable because it happened so long ago. Maybe it feels like a tale rather than a reality. But let's open our minds and look toward this story of Jesus, the Son of Man and Son of God.

This is the theme of Luke 1. Anticipation, a foreshadowing of what's to come. A hint. A clue. Just enough of the story to make us want to know more. God allows us to "rattle the gift" to give us a hint of joy and excitement. Ask yourself, *Where am I in this story?* and He will begin to give you clues of unimaginable gifts to which all the other gifts under the tree cannot compare!

Process
1. In what part of your life do you feel dark or alone?
2. Can you imagine light pouring in?
3. Ask God to give you the gift of hope and expectation this Christmas.

Prayer
Dear God, You are the Light of the World. Please remind me that when I'm in a relationship with You, I also can more brightly shine by reflecting You.

Promise
"He who is mightier than I is coming." (Luke 3:16)

Luke 2—Receive

For unto you is born this day in the city of David a Savior, who is Christ the Lord.

—Luke 2:11

The time had come. The day of all days had arrived. Joseph, a descendant of King David, and Mary, his fiancée, had returned to Bethlehem as required by the Roman emperor to register for the census. Likely exhausted after their long journey and unable to find lodging, they settled in with the animals and prepared for the birth of their baby. And then, finally, the Holy One arrived—a human, and yet as prophesied, the Son of God.

Mary wrapped Him in strips of cloth and laid Him in a manger, a feeding trough for the animals. And there He lay before them—a light in the darkness, the Savior, the Messiah, the Lord.

A host of angels appeared to the shepherds, praising God and proclaiming, "Glory to God in the highest, and on earth peace among those with whom he is pleased" (Luke 2:14).

In addition to the birth of Christ, peace is a predominant message of Christmas.

The angels were the first to announce that Jesus's arrival would offer a great gift—the gift of peace. The people of the world desire peace, but what does this mean to us? Peace is an inner sense of calm regardless of the outer circumstances and conflicts of life. This explains why beauty pageant contestants often answer "world peace" when asked what is the biggest need our world currently faces. Most agree that if someone offered us the gift of complete peace, of course, we would immediately accept.

Luke 2 also presents a number of characters entering the story of Jesus's birth in Bethlehem. What did they all have in common? They were human and longed for a Savior. As we peer into the story, we can learn from each individual's response. The first people who came in contact with Jesus were ready to receive their Lord. Let's look at how they reacted to the good news:

- The angels rejoiced and proclaimed glory to God.
- Mary pondered the birth of Jesus and watched the response of the people as they met her son, God's Son.
- Mary and Joseph presented and dedicated Him to the Lord.
- The shepherds glorified and praised God.
- Simeon, a righteous and devout man, proclaimed that salvation for the world had come through Jesus.
- Anna, a prophetess, gave thanks and told many.
- The teachers in the temple were amazed at Him.

Gifts are given at different times in the lives of individuals: birthdays, anniversaries, and other special events. But many think of Christmas as the most significant time for gift giving. It's the one time of year that those who celebrate simultaneously give and receive gifts. I remember as a young girl on Christmas morning, one of the most exciting parts of receiving gifts was sharing the excitement with my friends. "What did you get?" I would ask, and we would celebrate together.

On the night Jesus was born, the world received the greatest gift ever given—the gift of a Savior who would deliver them and bring them peace. The people had finally received what they so desired. What about you? Have you received our Savior and the peace He provides? Do you have the inner calm gifted to those who believe and receive Him? If so, let us share the good news with others.

Process
1. How might you personally receive the gift of Jesus this year during the Christmas season?
2. If you could picture a gift that God might give you, what do you see as you open it?
3. What is one thing you can do to find a calm spirit today?

Prayer
Jesus, may I not only receive You but also look to You daily as my Savior. I long for the inner calm gifted to those who believe. Thank You for providing this sense of peace that is always available to me. Give me a spirit of tranquility and harmony today.

Promise
"But to all who did receive him, who believed in his name, he gave the right to become children of God." (John 1:12)

Luke 3—Proclaim

The voice of one crying in the wilderness: "Prepare the way of the Lord, make his paths straight."

—Luke 3:4

One of the most exciting events surrounding the Olympics is the torch relay. The relay was first performed in 1936 in Berlin and has been a tradition ever since. The flame of the torch always originates in Olympia, Greece, then travels around the world, carried mostly by foot, before arriving at the destination of the Olympic games. The flame proclaims, or officially announces, *let the games begin.*

With the torch comes excitement and anticipation, which culminates at the opening ceremonies. The people of the world's countries then come together for the games.

The torchbearers usher in a significant event. You might think that the greatest event in the world's history—the coming of the Messiah—would be announced in a similar fashion. But in Luke 3, we see an unexpected torchbearer. In humble fashion, John the Baptist makes his entry into the Christmas story. He was first introduced in Luke 1, leaping in his mother Elizabeth's womb when entering the presence of Jesus. Conceived by a mother past childbearing age, John's life embodies this message of truth: "with God all things are possible" (Matthew 19:26).

But how could the life of a king begin so humbly? It might seem that a teenage mother, a stable full of animals, and John, the forerunner who lived in the wilderness eating locusts and wild honey,

7

were not befitting a king but again we see that God's plan was different and *all things are possible.*

As foretold in the Old Testament, John was, in fact, prophesied to be the torchbearer for Jesus. Both Isaiah and Malachi predicted, with assurance from God, that there would be a messenger announcing the coming of the Lord. "A voice cries: 'In the wilderness prepare the way of the LORD; make straight in the desert a highway for our God'" (Isaiah 40:3). And "Behold, I send my messenger, and he will prepare the way before me. And the Lord whom you seek will suddenly come to his temple; and the messenger of the covenant in whom you delight, behold, he is coming, says the LORD of hosts" (Malachi 3:1). Although it seemed impossible, the announcement glowed bright and clear. Hope was on the way. Light would pierce the darkness. The Son of God was about to appear.

> Every valley shall be filled,
>   and every mountain and hill shall be made low,
> and the crooked shall become straight,
>   and the rough places shall become level ways,
> and all flesh shall see the salvation of God. (Luke 3:5–6)

What valleys or mountains are we facing today? What crooked or rough places seem impossible to navigate? John proclaimed and prepared the way for someone who was and still is able to level life's mountains and straighten life's paths. He is our Lord and Savior, our Messiah, our Jesus. He provides access to God through Himself, and as a result, all things are truly possible.

Process
1.   What valleys or mountains are you facing today?
2.   What crooked or rough places seem impossible to navigate?

3. Ask God to be your guide. Thank Him for His promise to do so.

Prayer

Almighty God, I have valleys and mountains that I am facing today. These crooked and rough places seem impossible to navigate. Thank You for leveling my life's mountains and straightening my life's paths. You are my Lord and Savior who provides access to God the Father through whom all things are possible.

Promise

"Behold, your king is coming to you." (Zechariah 9:9)

Luke 4—Believe

The Spirit of the Lord is upon me,
 because he has anointed me
 to proclaim good news to the poor.
He has sent me to proclaim liberty to the captives
 and recovering of sight to the blind,
 to set at liberty those who are oppressed,
to proclaim the year of the Lord's favor.

—Luke 4:18–19

The word *believe* seems to pop up everywhere at Christmastime: it's painted on wooden signs in red and green, it covers an ornament on the tree, or it's written in bold script across the front of a Christmas card. In our society's terms this may mean, "Do you believe in Santa Claus and his reindeer?" But in a deeper, spiritual sense, these reminders challenge us personally to believe in Jesus, celebrate His birth, and live in a way that demonstrates our belief.

In Luke 4, the ministry of Jesus began when He returned to Nazareth, his boyhood home, and went to the synagogue on the Sabbath (v. 16). Taking the scroll handed to Him, He stood to read the Scriptures. This seemed to be His first opportunity to publicly teach. It appears He intentionally chose to read a passage from Isaiah that prophesied His coming. In essence He said, "You have believed this. Now it is coming true right before your very eyes." *He* fulfilled the prophecy. Fulfill means "to carry out or bring to realization; to satisfy." Not everyone realized Isaiah's prophecy was being fulfilled, but those who did and believed that Jesus was the Son of God would be saved.

In fact, the passage tells us that when He finished reading, He sat down, and "the eyes of all in the synagogue were fixed on him" (v. 20). They probably could have heard a pin drop. Astonished, they were also likely curious and might have been thinking, *Could this really be the promised Messiah? Can we believe He will save us?*

Belief. This is a tenet on which the Christian faith stands. As a person who was raised in a Christian family, I can say I always believed in Jesus as my Savior. But because of the familiarity, the truth of what this meant became, at times, ineffective in my life.

You may have heard the tale of one fish who said to the other, "How's the water today?" The second fish responded, "What's water?" This could be true of me as a seasoned believer. I had grown so accustomed to the faith that I ceased to appreciate the abundant life Christ had for me. I trusted that the Bible was God's Word, and I had put my faith in Him, but often I wasn't living like I truly believed. I didn't feel the daily freedom and joy He offered. I would have considered Jesus's teaching in Luke 4 as directed toward an unbeliever, not myself.

Later in my adult life, after a reconversion of sorts, I began to recognize that even though I believed in God, my life did not show evidence. When we genuinely believe the truth of God's Word, our lives will be filled with peace, hope, love, joy, and freedom. He came to offer us a fulfilling life. Jesus says in John 10:10, "I came that they may have life and have it abundantly."

And what about the most familiar verse in the Bible? "For God so loved the world, that he gave his only Son, that whoever believes in him should not perish but have eternal life" (John 3:16).

The good news about Jesus applies to us not only on the day we first trusted Christ but also right here and now, wherever we find ourselves. The gospel is unending truth for everyone who chooses to believe. What about us? Do we see the gospel as:

- providing good news when we feel we have none?
- granting freedom from what holds us captive?
- giving sight in areas where we are unable to clearly see?

Every part of the message that Jesus proclaimed remains current and relevant for those of us who believe and put our trust in Him. If our lives are filled with depression, fear, anxiety, guilt, or shame, let us either recommit our lives to Jesus or put our hope in Him for the first time. As we look at the manger, may it always be a reminder of the hope we have in Jesus.

Process
1. What are you struggling to believe today?
2. Recommit to God any parts of your life that are filled with depression, fear, anxiety, guilt, or shame.
3. What do you know to be true about God?

Prayer
Dear Father, the gospel provides me with unending truth when I choose to believe. Help me find the good news that You promise to provide when I feel I have none. Grant me freedom from what holds me captive. I'm grateful that You will give me sight in areas where I am unable to clearly see.

Promise
"All this took place to fulfill what the Lord had spoken by the prophet." (Matthew 1:22)

Luke 5—Heal

And the power of the Lord was with him to heal.
—Luke 5:17

Not today, I woke up thinking. As a small girl just before a dreaded dentist appointment, I began to worry as soon as I opened my eyes. I despised going to the dentist because of any possibility of pain or discomfort. Anxiety bubbled up inside. But walking into the waiting room at the dentist's office, I was quickly distracted by a children's magazine called *Highlights*. It sat on the coffee table waiting for me. My favorite activity within the magazine was called "Hidden Pictures," similar to today's "Where's Waldo." I'd grab a pen from my mother's purse and begin my search, finding and circling little objects that were hidden in larger pictures. The hunt for those objects kept my mind busy, keeping away the fear about what might happen in the scary dentist's chair.

As Jesus continued His brief but extensive ministry of teaching and healing while walking the earth, He lived and spoke in hidden pictures. In Luke 5, Jesus begins to teach using parables—stories with hidden meanings. While we find a number of these stories in the New Testament, we have no idea how many hundreds of stories He must have told that weren't recorded. His way of communicating with people had them searching, questioning, and marveling at how eloquently and creatively He spoke the truth. The parables were always coupled with lessons—some overt, some less obvious—and have been defined as "earthly stories with heavenly

13

meanings." Simply put, they are analogies. The people leaned in and listened, enthralled. Jesus then told the story and concluded it with a brief but profound truth. There was deep meaning hidden within each story, meanings that still apply to us today.

All of Jesus's ministry on earth had profound meaning, not just His parables. For example, after a fisherman named Simon had fished all night and caught nothing, Jesus told him to cast his net again. The nets filled with so many fish that the boat almost sank. Jesus used this miracle to explain to the fishermen that if they followed Him they would soon be "catching men," or bringing men to know Him. Most every act and word during Jesus's time on earth explained a truth He was sent to proclaim.

There is more to learn, and there are more hidden pictures in Luke 5 when Jesus healed the sick, the lame, and the diseased, and when He raised people from the dead. Why did He heal people and raise people from the dead? In verse 23 Jesus says, "Which is easier, to say, 'Your sins are forgiven you,' or to say, 'Rise and walk'?" Not only did He have love and compassion for the people, but they also needed to see His great power in order to believe that He was the Son of God. "But for you who fear my name, the sun of righteousness shall rise with healing in its wings. You shall go out leaping like calves from the stall" (Malachi 4:2).

The great power of Jesus was seen when He arrived in one of the villages and was met by a man who had leprosy. Upon seeing Jesus, the man "fell on his face and begged him, 'Lord, if you will, you can make me clean.' And Jesus stretched out his hand and touched him, saying, 'I will; be clean.' And immediately the leprosy left him" (Luke 5:12–13). Jesus reached out and touched this man who was considered unclean with a highly contagious and advanced disease. Jesus didn't avoid him or shun him; instead He showed compassion and healed him. Although we are sinful and broken, He forgives us, loves us, and offers us spiritual healing.

There is so much about the life of Christ that we will not understand until we get to heaven, but for now we can see that the healing of the physically sick was a precursor to the spiritual healing of His people. Jesus offered the gift of grace—the free and unmerited favor of God. We are all in need of help and healing as we live in a world full of sin and death. God is the ultimate Healer. He reaches out and touches us when we are hurting and broken. He comes with healing in His wings, as Malachi said.

The fact is not hidden and not difficult to see that we all need a refuge, a shelter, a haven. We all need healing. Since Jesus came to earth, we now have access to the Father, who offers us all of these things. When we read or hear the stories of Jesus healing the sick and raising the dead, may we be reminded of the hidden pictures in our own lives and never forget that He has the power to protect us and to heal us. Let us stand in awe of the greatest gift He brings at Christmas . . . *the gift of life.*

Process

1. In what way do you feel needy or weak today?
2. Reflect on a time God helped or rescued you.
3. Thank God that He can be trusted as your refuge, shelter, and healer.

Prayer

God, I need healing, sometimes physically but many times emotionally and spiritually. May I feel You reaching out and touching me when I am hurt and broken. May I see You coming to my rescue with healing and restoration.

Promise
"With his wounds we are healed." (Isaiah 53:5)

Luke 6—Hunger

And he lifted up his eyes on his disciples, and said: . . .
"Blessed are you who are hungry now, for you shall be
satisfied."

—Luke 6:20–21

One particular year, in the midst of the hustle and bustle of Christmas, the demands of life took priority over my time to focus on the birth of Christ. My son and I were visiting and catching up. When he asked how I was doing, I expressed frustration about not having enough time to read, pray, and reflect on the season. I told him that, as a result, my spirit felt disconnected from Advent. In the past, I'd always felt guilty when not praying, meditating, or reading daily devotionals. But at this middle stage of life, rather than feel guilty, I'd developed a sense of imbalance. I felt my life was not centered properly without the truth about who I was in Christ, the freedom He offered, and the opportunity to humble myself before Him. I longed to daily reconnect with Him so I could continue to discover the person He desired me to be. This only happened when I was in a consistent, close relationship with Him.

As I expressed frustration to my son, he responded with kindness rather than judgment. He said something like, "Mom, there will always be times we don't get to be with God as much as we'd like. These are the times to feel our hunger, realize our need in a deeper way, and respond with the attitude of longing to understand more clearly the importance of Jesus." In other words, *feel the hunger more deeply!* There's that word *longing* again. Longing, in the spiritual sense, means desiring Jesus.

In Luke 6, Jesus began to help the newly appointed apostles understand the importance of embracing brokenness. Years ago, I remember hearing in church the words, "Pray for brokenness." *Yikes*, I thought. I don't want God to break me by taking me to a place of hurt and pain. But we are all broken, hurt, and hungry for a Savior. We all need to understand that He came to the world to bring forgiveness and healing. And the healing started with the baby in a manger, thousands of years ago when God sent His Son to earth in human form.

Our relationship with Him heals, completes, and sustains us as we live in a world where brokenness, sickness, and hurt abound. Trusting His ways, His plans, and His love brings the ultimate fulfillment. He alone can satisfy our longing.

Luke 6 explains that embracing our own emptiness results in inheriting all God has to offer. We see this concept in the eight Beatitudes, or blessings. This is where our longings are met and our hunger satisfied. This is where we see Him, our all-sufficient God. If we turn to Him with tears, our caring Father will provide comfort and wipe them away. Because our identity rests in Him, when we are filled with conflict and rejection He will restore us as His children and right all wrongs. He is the one who saves us; He is our ultimate Redeemer. We, as His children, live inside the gates of a lavish kingdom.

When we feel poor and powerless, He completes us. "But he said to me, 'My grace is sufficient for you, for my power is made perfect in weakness.' Therefore I will boast all the more gladly of my weaknesses, so that the power of Christ may rest upon me. For the sake of Christ, then, I am content with weaknesses, insults, hardships, persecutions, and calamities. For when I am weak, then I am strong" (2 Corinthians 12:9–10).

When we feel hungry for more, He fills us. "And my God will supply every need of yours according to his riches in glory in Christ Jesus" (Philippians 4:19).

When we feel sad, He wipes away our tears. "For we do not have a high priest who is unable to sympathize with our weaknesses, but one who in every respect has been tempted as we are, yet without sin" (Hebrews 4:15).

When we feel rejected, He understands. He's been there.

He was despised and rejected by men,
  a man of sorrows and acquainted with grief;
and as one from whom men hide their faces
  he was despised, and we esteemed him not. (Isaiah 53:3)

And if we're in a relationship with Him, we will be blessed. Here again we see the reason for Christmas and His coming to earth—not only to sustain us in weakness but also to teach us the way to satisfy our hunger by finding nourishment through life in Him.

Process
1. What are your deepest longings?
2. In what ways do you feel weak?
3. Thank God that He has been right where you are and understands your needs and how to feed your hunger.

Prayer
Lord, my relationship with You completes me as I live in a world where brokenness, sickness, and hurt abound. I often seem to forget

that I can trust Your ways, Your plans, and Your goodness. Help me remember that Your nourishment brings the ultimate fulfillment and You alone can satisfy my deepest longings.

Promise
"Blessed are those who hunger and thirst for righteousness, for they shall be satisfied." (Matthew 5:6)

Luke 7—Feel

And when the Lord saw her, he had compassion on her and said to her, "Do not weep."

—Luke 7:13

Not long ago, we took a trip to Fairhope in our home state of Alabama. Fairhope lies on the east bank of Mobile Bay, which feeds the Gulf of Mexico. We stayed at the historic Grand Hotel, which is built in a picturesque beach hamlet called Point Clear and is surrounded by huge oak trees dripping with Spanish moss. The rooms have private balconies on which you can sit in rocking chairs and see for miles out over the bay.

One evening we were sitting on our balcony, rocking, decompressing, and taking in the coast and its salty air when we heard a small boy's voice screaming with jubilation. His big screams of excitement were followed by his little frame running across the grass toward the end of the property. Not far behind came his parents slowly strolling, maybe on a walk after dinner. In my heart, I joined the little boy thinking, *Yes, I agree! It's so beautiful I could scream!* He was saying, "Look! Can you see any fish? Can we go swimming tomorrow? Woo-hoo!" As he ran circles around his parents, he yelled at the top of his lungs, "This is the best day!" We watched them continue down the boardwalk until they were out of sight and his precious voice faded into the salty air.

Ten minutes later we heard the same little voice cry out, "But I want to get ice cream!" The daddy told him no, and the little guy began to weep. He proceeded to throw himself down on the grass, sobbing and begging, "Please, Daddy!" The parents kept walking and calling him to come with them, but he refused to get up. He had made up his mind; he wanted ice cream. He continued to beg and beg and beg, and I worried that his dad would lose his temper and reprimand him. I feared what was coming. I thought, *Please get up, little boy, because my heart will be sad if you get in trouble.*

Holding my breath, I continued to watch. The daddy finally turned around and approached his small son, who was now flailing on the grass. He stooped down, wrapped his big daddy arms around the little boy, picked him up, and brought him close to his warm body. He said, "I see that you are mad, and yes, it would be fun to get ice cream. But tonight we can't. Maybe tomorrow. It's been a long day, and you need your rest." The kindness in his voice coupled with his embrace made the boy relax and melt into his father's loving arms.

Luke 7 brings us stories of the tenderness of Jesus. There are narratives of people who were in great need. They were sick and wounded, lame and hurting—even to the point of death. They were sinful and needed forgiveness. In verse 16, after Jesus had raised a young man from the dead, the crowd acknowledged, "God has visited His people!"

We see Jesus healing people by physically touching them. He could have simply spoken a word of healing over them, but instead, He chose to reach out to them. It must have been overwhelming to His followers that their God was now in human form, standing beside them. Soon, they would no longer be required to approach Him in the temple with a priest's help and an animal sacrifice. They could actually go to Him themselves. He welcomed everyone. Jesus's touch was a tangible way for His people to feel His unconditional acceptance: children, lepers, even a sinful woman who entered a stranger's house to wash Jesus's feet. Luke tells us that she washed His feet with her tears, dried them with her hair, kissed them, and put expensive perfume on them. What a beautiful picture of love. One Pharisee said to himself, "If this man were a prophet, he would have known who and what sort of woman this is who is touching him, for she is a sinner" (v. 39). Jesus answered his thought by praising the woman for showing Him such love and explaining that He welcomed her. Jesus then told the woman, "Your sins are forgiven. . . . Your faith has saved you; go in peace" (vv. 48, 50).

This is our Jesus. He draws near to us, despite our sin. He calls us to reach out for Him in our darkest moments. This is Him showing us grace, giving us a gift we don't deserve.

Think back to the father of the little boy who threw a fit at the Grand Hotel. He loved his child so much that he didn't admonish him in his moment of rebellion. Like Jesus does for us, he forgave him, reached down, scooped him up, and simply loved him.

Process
1. In what ways do you need comfort today?
2. Can you picture God forgiving your sin and offering grace?
3. Ask God to allow you to feel loved by Him like never before.

Prayer
God, as a sinner, sometimes it's hard for me to draw near to You. May I hear You calling to me in my darkest moments. Your light shows me grace, giving me an undeserved gift for which I'm grateful.

Promise
"As one whom his mother comforts,
  so I will comfort you." (Isaiah 66:13)

Luke 8—Declare

And he went away, proclaiming throughout the whole city how much Jesus had done for him.

—Luke 8:39

Many of the chapters in Luke mirror one another. Jesus's life was filled with building relationships, teaching, telling stories, healing, and returning life to the dead. All these ways of relating to the people showed Him as not only the promised Savior but also a personal God. Each chapter tells similar stories of Jesus walking with people on the road, preaching in their places of worship, dining with them in their homes, and teaching them through parables. We find people pouring out their hearts to Him and begging for His help. From debilitating physical infirmities to painful interpersonal conflicts to severe mental illnesses, we see brokenness, pain, and grief. In chapter 8 we see Jesus offering life in place of death, healing in place of sickness, and hope in place of hopelessness. And all the while, He exudes a spirit of love.

In the beginning of the chapter, the template of Jesus's life is simply stated. "He went on through cities and villages, proclaiming and bringing the good news of the kingdom of God. And the twelve were with him, and also some women who had been healed of evil spirits and infirmities" (vv. 1–2).

The people had begun to proclaim the good news and word was spreading fast. Throughout this chapter, a common thread weaves together the voices of each person Jesus touched. His message goes out through each of them as they declare, proclaim, and tell those around them what He has done.

Luke tells a story about the disciples crossing a lake with Jesus when a storm whipped up, almost sinking their boat. Fearing the danger and scared they might drown, the disciples woke Jesus from His nap. He rebuked the wind and waves, calming the storm. In the next story, Jesus cast out multiple demons from an insane man. With Jesus's permission, the demons possessed a herd of pigs, which plunged off a steep hillside into a lake and drowned. Not surprisingly, "When the herdsmen saw what had happened, they fled and told it in the city and in the country" (v. 34). Although the cured man wanted to stay with Jesus, He told him, "Return to your home, and declare how much God has done for you" (v. 39). Next, as Jesus made His way through a crowd toward a sick young girl, He sensed someone had touched His robe. When He felt healing power go out from Him, He asked His disciples, "Who was it that touched me?" (v. 45). In fear, a sick woman admitted she had reached for Him in hopes of being healed, and indeed she had been healed. Jesus responded, "Daughter, your faith has made you well. Go in peace" (v. 48). He then continued His trek toward the sick girl but was told she had died. But Jesus took her by the hand, commanded her to get up, and raised her from the dead.

Both the woman and the girl were touched by Jesus and given new life. The woman "declared in the presence of all the people" her need for Jesus (v. 47). Many people witnessed these miracles, and word began to spread.

Imagine similar stories today. We hear about soldiers who have returned from war with devastating injuries but somehow manage to create unbelievable lives for themselves and their families. We hear about athletes who have been seriously injured, with no hope of returning to their sport but somehow completely recover. We hear about people who are diagnosed with cancer and given a poor prognosis only to outlive the doctor's prediction by many years with a productive life. We rejoice when those we love are healed, and we want to share their stories: "Did you hear about her? Did you see him on the news? How exciting—what an unbelievable comeback!"

I once heard about an elderly woman who lived out her final years in a nursing home. She could hardly hear, see, or speak. But she was a woman of faith, who leaned on God during her times of hardship. She reached a point where she could only mumble two words. These were the only words she spoke for the last year of her life. To anyone with whom she came into contact, she whispered, "He can." Oh what joy is offered to those who believe that *He can*. The news is so good that it's hard to keep it to ourselves. Let us marvel at what He has done. Let's declare, proclaim, and tell others what God is doing!

What about you? Has God been so faithful at times that you couldn't hold it in? You just had to share it with someone? Or maybe you haven't personally experienced a miracle but you would like to. This Christmas let's ask God for the ability to see what He is doing in our lives, then let's go out and tell the world what we have seen!

Process
1. Name one person who points you back to God.
2. Are you a person who knows the truth and shares it with others?
3. Ask God for a miracle or message of hope that you can share with someone today.

Prayer

God, when I see You offering healing in place of sickness, hope in place of hopelessness, and life in place of death, I feel so grateful. May this gratitude for all that You've done for me spill over on those around me. As I receive Your grace, may I become a source of grace for others because of Your unconditional love for me.

Promise

"With God all things are possible." (Matthew 19:26)

Luke 9—Retreat

He took with him Peter and John and James and went up on the mountain to pray.

—Luke 9:28

Do you ever feel like life is too difficult to handle? Sometimes there seems to be too much required of us, and we can't get it done. We exhaust ourselves working hard to check off our long to-do lists, but they never seem to get any shorter. Additionally, we always seem to need a raise or a bonus, another educational degree, or just more hours in our day. It's almost impossible to turn off the voices of the world that shout, "Be successful! Be more! You can have it all if you'll just work a little harder, go a little faster, be a little smarter."

And then, if that isn't enough, sometimes we are surrounded by people who expect more of us than we have to give. Despair or depression can result from the demands of providing for a family, caring for an ailing loved one, or struggling to hold a marriage together. We might be thinking, *Why can't things settle down just a bit?* or *When will life get back to normal?* But as soon as things settle, along comes another struggle, like a freight train off in the distance: it's coming fast, and you can't slow it down.

In Luke 9, we meet the disciples, a band of boys—some only teenagers—and young men. They seem energetic and excited, expectant and sometimes overly eager. A life of following Jesus was coming at a fast pace. Jesus's followers swarmed around them seeking miracles, healing, truth, and comfort. On this day, a crowd of five thousand men, along with their families, had followed Jesus, seeking His teaching and healing. The day had turned into evening, and the people needed to eat. Jesus's disciples wanted to send them away to find food and lodging, but Jesus had a better idea. After blessing the only food they had—five loaves and two fish—Jesus broke the bread, and His disciples distributed the food until all were filled. This was just one example of a day with Jesus. The masses of people had been waiting and their need for a Savior had been building for generations. They hoped and believed the prophecy that He was coming. To say that their longings needed satiating would be an understatement. Their souls were starving for a God who would provide emotional rest, and they had grown desperate.

Hope stood before them in the person of Jesus. The disciples were busy casting out evil spirits, healing people, and proclaiming the kingdom of God (vv. 1–6). But these young world changers had a limited view of the true needs of the people. Jesus, however, understood both their physical and spiritual needs. He could see into the hearts of those who surrounded Him most everywhere He went, and He knew their souls needed nourishment. They needed rest from their inner turmoil. The responsibility must have felt enormous. He was human, so He had emotions and felt things deeply, like we do. Yet He was also God and had the ability to see into the heart of each individual.

Can you imagine the emotional weight He must have felt? How did He carry the burdens of thousands on His shoulders? Yes, He was God, but although it's difficult to understand, He also had the limitations of a man. For this reason, He can relate to us and our daily challenges.

Jesus continued to speak to His friends, the disciples, with teachings that were overwhelming, even impossible. In this chapter we read verses like, "Deny himself and take up his cross daily and follow me" (v. 23). "Whoever would save his life will lose it" (v. 24). "No one who puts his hand to the plow and looks back is fit for the kingdom of God" (v. 62). As if meeting the overwhelming needs of the people wasn't hard enough for the disciples, Jesus came out with statements like these. Our temptation might be to skip over these directives that Jesus spoke and move on thinking, *I can never do that.*

But Jesus was preparing the disciples—and us. The Bible tells us, "He remembers that we are dust" (Psalm 103:14). He knows we can't live up to His perfect law, because as humans, we are not capable. In the events that follow, Jesus introduces us to His Holy Spirit, who will enable us to do what He is asking, will comfort us along the way, and will help us have faith. His Spirit will never leave us alone. In our times of great need and hunger, His Spirit completes us. By giving us the impossible commands found in chapter 9, Jesus set the stage for how we are to live with complete dependence on Him. He told the people in John 14:6, "I am the way, and the truth, and the life."

Jesus continually modeled for His followers a life that is lived under the love and leading of His heavenly Father. He seemed to say, *This is how it's done.* He showed us how to live with all of the stress and demands that at times seem overwhelming. Luke 9 gives three instances where He retreated from the crowds. In verse 10, Jesus "withdrew." In verse 18, we observe Him "praying alone." And in verse 28, He invited some of the disciples up "on the mountain to pray." He retreated often. Pulling back and connecting with His heavenly Father is seen over and over throughout Jesus's journey on earth. Disengaging with the people allowed Him to engage with God, His Father.

Jesus has given us the recipe for the secret sauce. This is the way to handle the demands surrounding us and how we find solace when our burdens exhaust and overwhelm. Retreat. Find rest. Find enablement, empowerment, and encouragement in the God who loves us and promises to meet our every need.

This Christmas let us celebrate Jesus, who has shown us the way to have an intimate connection with God our Father. Retreat, pray, and listen. He is waiting for us.

Process
1.　What swirling demands are causing you to feel stressed?
2.　On a scale of 1 to 10, how tired are you today?
3.　Do you see connecting with God as a place of rest?

Prayer
May I more intentionally celebrate You, Jesus, this Christmas. You have shown me the way, through You, to have an intimate connection with God, our Father. Remind me to retreat, pray, and listen to Your voice. I'm so moved that You are always waiting for me to come and spend time with You.

Promise
"But they who wait for the LORD shall renew their strength." (Isaiah 40:31)

Luke 10—Hope

He went to him and bound up his wounds, pouring on oil and wine. Then he set him on his own animal and brought him to an inn and took care of him.

—Luke 10:34

A curious baby crawls down a hallway. As he crawls along, the hallway gets darker. Frightened, he turns his chubby cheeks and looks behind him. Suddenly, he doesn't like the dark. He feels unsafe. He lets out a cry as if to say, *Help me! It's dark in here and I'm alone!* Quickly, in his insecurity, he heads back toward the light, toward the hope of help, of safety—salvation.

Throughout the New Testament, people turned to Jesus, recognizing Him as a source of light and help. Who could blame them? Everywhere He went, He taught, healed, and simply spent time with people. He built relationships woven with grace, truth, and love. His followers began to spread the news that the Messiah who had come to save His people was now living among them.

No wonder people sought His help when they were in His presence, not only for His teaching but also for ordinary things, such as abundant food (Luke 9) or wine (John 2). When sisters Mary and Martha welcomed Jesus and His disciples into their home, they rejoiced in their ability to offer hospitality, and Martha busied herself working to prepare a meal for the large group. When Mary sat at Jesus's feet, absorbing His every word, Martha complained,

"Lord, doesn't it seem unfair to you that my sister just sits here while I do all the work? Tell her to come and help me."

But Jesus did not tell Mary to help her sister. Instead he explained, "My dear Martha, you are worried and upset over all these details! There is only one thing worth being concerned about. Mary has discovered it, and it will not be taken away from her."

What an inspiring picture, especially during the days leading up to Christmas when we are busy finding the perfect gift, cooking for many people, and attending so many holiday celebrations. But on the contrary, Jesus invites us to slow down and sit at His feet. He desires for us to look past the details of the season and listen to and worship Him as we celebrate His birth.

In Luke 10, Jesus tells the story of the good Samaritan. My memories take me back to children's church when I heard this story for the first time. It's a story about a traveler who was robbed and beaten and left to die. Lying in a ditch, in desperation he watched as passersby, including two men of the cloth, chose to look the other way rather than help him. Hopeless, he watched several people walk down the far side of the road, ignoring his desperate state. But then, a Samaritan noticed him. He was drawn to him. He helped him by offering medical aid and finding a place for him to stay. He carried the helpless traveler to safety. He bought food and more to meet the wounded, weary man's needs. He essentially gave him hope in the midst of a frightening situation.

The moral of the story has been widely accepted as helping others. Go out of your way. Reach out to those who are different. Make sacrifices. Show love and care even when it's inconvenient or uncomfortable.

But let's look at this story from a different perspective. Instead of putting ourselves in the place of the helper, the good Samaritan, let's imagine ourselves as the man who needs help. We likely know how he felt, because at times, life can really kick us into the ditch. While we might not be physically wounded, we all know about rejection and hurt. Sometimes it feels like we are crawling down a dark hallway alone. Insecurity creeps in. *Is anyone there? Will anyone help me?* We cry out to God, "Is there any hope in this situation?"

God sometimes allows us to remain in a desperate state much longer than we think we can bear. Anxious for hope and healing, we want Him to rescue us quickly, but sometimes it takes a few hours, days, or even more. We wonder, *Why are You leaving me alone and insecure? Are You even out there?* We don't always know His reasons for allowing us to remain in what feels like a ditch, but the Bible does tell us amazing things about God's timing. His children are often waiting, longing, and hoping that they will see His kindness and goodness through His provision. But we also see that He will rescue us because He is our good Samaritan. And because we have stories of our own about how He has rescued us, we are able to go out and help others. His past faithfulness paves the way for our future faith. So we hope and are confident, by faith, that He is coming to rescue us. And as He has promised, He will come. His timing is perfect. Just give it one more hour, one more day, or maybe even longer.

The world waited hundreds of years for Jesus, and He arrived at the perfect time. He came to rescue, heal, feed, and shelter His children. This is the reason we have hope that one day, some day, we will be rescued from the ditch by our Savior, and we will rejoice again. No matter how dark or alone we might feel, let's turn back to our Father, God, believing in His rescue and trusting that His timing is best.

Process

Fill in the blank:

1. I hope _____.
2. I need _____.
3. God, please give me the gift of _____.

Prayer

Father, sometimes it's hard for me to believe in Your goodness. Remind me that Your past faithfulness paves the way for my future faith. I hope and am confident, by faith, that You are coming to rescue me. Just as promised, You will come. Your timing is perfect. Help me to trust You more.

Promise

"Our soul waits for the LORD;
  he is our help and our shield." (Psalm 33:20)

Luke 11—Inherit

*For everyone who asks receives, and the one who seeks
finds, and to the one who knocks it will be opened.*

—Luke 11:10

It was the late 1980s, and we were a couple of twentysomething
interior decorator wannabes starting families of our own. My sister and I loved heading out together to estate sales around town,
hoping to find the next treasure for the homes that we were creat-
ing. Even a trip to the thrift store, where we would find the perfect
lamp or end table, delighted us. Wherever we went, it was not only
about being frugal but also about the hunt, the find, the prize! We
wondered where each piece had been, and we knew we would hear
quite a story if these pieces could talk. We love furnishings that
have meaning or memories tucked deep within.

Years ago, we received a phone call from Georgia. Our great
aunt Gigi had been notified by a local storage company that
they were permanently closing their doors and all units must be
vacated. At first, she had no idea why they were calling her, but
then she remembered that many years before, she had moved her
parents out of their home on Tybee Island and had rented a storage unit in which to house their furniture. But years and years
and years had passed, and she'd never needed the furniture. Now
she lived in a retirement home and, of course, had nowhere to put
it, so she kindly thought of my sister and me.

"Would y'all be interested in driving over and taking whatever furniture you want from that storage unit? I don't have much recollection of what's in there, but if it's worth the drive, come on. It's all yours." Without hesitation, we rented a truck and were on our way to the greatest treasure hunt of our lives! We talked and dreamed and guessed what treasures might fill that unit. We knew the furniture had come from a large southern home on the island, surrounded by live oaks dripping with Spanish moss.

As you may have guessed, it was worth the trip! We cracked open the doors of the unit and the lovely smell of years gone by enveloped us. We were thrilled! It felt like we had hit the jackpot. Both of us went home from that trip with many family heirlooms, knowing that the rich family heritage we so greatly valued would soon fill our homes.

In Luke 11, Jesus's disciples found Him praying. As His prayer time came to a close, one disciple asked Him to teach them how to pray. He responded by providing an example of prayer—The Lord's Prayer. He indicated that the temple and priest were no longer necessary for His followers to be in relationship with Him. It was as if He were saying, "I'm always available for you," words we all want to hear from someone we love. The prayer also included adoration of God, dependence on Him, confession of sins, and grace, or unmerited favor. How kind He must have seemed as He extended this invitation to communicate with God through prayer.

But He went a step further. He told the story of a visitor who went to a neighbor's house one night needing bread. The visitor kept incessantly knocking until he woke his neighbor. Jesus seemed to be saying, "You can come to me for anything, anytime." I think of the word *intimate*. He was telling them to come close. The Bible tells us, "Draw near to God, and he will draw near to you" (James 4:8). It also says of God, "You . . . are acquainted with all my ways" (Psalm 139:3).

My sister and I urgently and expectantly opened the door of the storage unit because we believed treasures we were to inherit awaited us. And we were correct! Likewise, Jesus invited His people to come close, knock urgently, and expect great things from Him. He wanted them—and He wants us—to be thrilled with the treasures He brings: faith, hope, love, and salvation, to name a few.

As we open gifts this Christmas, may they remind us of God's invitation to draw near and see how He welcomes and accepts us, just as we are. As a child of the King, our inheritance stretches beyond imagination. He has storehouses filled with rich blessings that await His children. May we be amazed and overwhelmed with joy when we receive the gifts that He offers us through a personal relationship with Him.

Process

1. What's the best gift you remember receiving?
2. Have you ever received an unexpected gift from God?
3. What are some of the gifts God gives you through His Son?

Prayer

God, I see Jesus inviting Your people to come close, knock urgently, and expect great things from Him. You invite me to do the same. Thrill me with Your many treasures—faith, hope, love, and salvation, to name just a few. Thank You for offering me abundant life through Your Son, Jesus.

Promise

"The lines have fallen for me in pleasant places;
  indeed, I have a beautiful inheritance." (Psalm 16:6)

Luke 12—Pursue

Seek his kingdom, and these things will be added to you.
—Luke 12:31

Here we are, nearly at the halfway point in this book of Luke. With the flip of each page, the story builds, and we move from curious and tentative to confident and excited. The words become more personal, and we are drawn in. As we get to know this Jesus of Nazareth, we feel welcomed and inspired. How overwhelmed those who witnessed His life firsthand must have felt! The disciples, as well as the crowds who followed Jesus, had to be both amazed and confused at this very different, very young man who was approachable and mysterious, divisive and powerful.

Luke 12 opens with an enormous crowd congregating: "so many thousands of the people had gathered together that they were trampling one another" (v. 1). Many translations of the Bible use the word *trample*. Trampling implies urgency and confusion resulting in a potentially harmful situation. What would cause people to trample one another? Why would they take such a risk in order to see and hear Jesus?

Can you imagine the scene that likely unfolded most every day of Jesus's life? Picture an eager, even frantic crowd trying to get into a popular musician's concert or fans rushing into a competitive sporting event. Or what about a helicopter landing in a country where people depended on the water and food it brought?

The words of Jesus in chapter 12 seem to provide reasons for the trampling. He offered people a new, different way to live, a way not bound by the stringent rules of law. He spoke about freedom through a warm relationship with a personal Savior. He was God in the flesh. They must have been enamored and drawn to Him and, as a result, driven in their pursuit of Him. Next we read about power over fear. They didn't need to be afraid, Jesus explained. They didn't need to worry. He reminded them how God even valued the sparrows. He told them that God had numbered every hair on their heads! He made sure they understood that God deeply cared for each of them like a loving father cares for his child. Just a taste of this compelling message made them want more and more. This is why they were willing to risk everything to hear from Jesus.

But some of the truths we read in this chapter are not so pleasant. He admonished those who focused on religion and spiritual to-do lists rather than their relationship with God. He warned people of the consequences of denying Him in front of others. But the most challenging call seemed to be when He said in verse 15, "One's life does not consist in the abundance of his possessions." *Wow*, they must have thought. *We've had it all wrong!* Who doesn't long for peace, comfort, and a better life by obtaining more material possessions? This couldn't have been a popular message, but still, the crowds kept coming back to hear more.

So why would they risk being trampled to pursue learning about these challenging, even contrary new truths? In addition to their curiosity, there must have been a mysterious and unexplained force drawing them toward Jesus. It was as if a doctor had given them a horrible diagnosis, but in the next breath, he offered them a cure. The message seemed counterintuitive. They wanted a greater understanding of His teachings and this new mindset that

He was the Son of God in the flesh. They were ready not only to say, "I'm all in," but also to *force* their way in. They were beginning to understand that the freedom, hope, and healing that had been promised in the Old Testament four hundred years earlier were now available to them. It was worth trampling in order to get to Jesus and all He offered. Suddenly, with His presence on earth, it was as if their lives depended on getting close to Him and the joy and peace He brought.

As we see people this holiday season compete for the most sought-after presents, let's imagine ourselves in the crowd of those who were pushing and trampling in order to see and hear Jesus. While shoppers fight for the best gifts, may we remember that the perfect gift comes from Jesus. Let us understand the significance of the beautiful relationship with Him that awaits us and wake every morning ready to trample our distractions. With a sense of urgency, let's pursue Him, the God who is always there for us.

Process

1. In what new way do you see Jesus as you read Luke's Gospel?
2. Do you see yourself as desperately seeking God?
3. How can you pursue God in your places of need?

Prayer

Dear Father, I want to live each day as if my life depends on Your presence. Give me the joy and peace that are available when I have a greater awareness that You are near. Will You show me Yourself in a new and powerful way today?

Promise

"You will seek me and find me, when you seek me with all your heart." (Jeremiah 29:13)

Luke 13—Nestle

*How often would I have gathered your children together
as a hen gathers her brood under her wings.*

—Luke 13:34

Today, December 13, we find ourselves in Luke 13, halfway into the story of Jesus's short life on earth. The plot surrounding Him thickens. As we continue, let us be curious, amazed, and ready to receive this gift of Jesus. An unexpected, undefinable, unbelievable offering is headed our way. At this midpoint, may we draw near to Him as He lovingly pursues us. You may currently believe in God, or you may have believed in Him in the past, but now He seems distant. You might be considering for the first time putting your trust in God. Wherever you find yourself on the journey, this is your opportunity to look to Him and say, "I want more of You."

Having tried many unfulfilling things in the past to bring happiness, some of us may feel empty and insecure. We may feel overwhelmed with worry, sadness, or guilt. This could be the beginning of telling God that we need Him. We can't make it without Him. He knows that our trust in Him is frail and laced with struggle. He knows that we're tired of fighting to live a fulfilling life. He knows that we don't think we are enough. So the stage is set. He is ready to provide meaning when we feel meaningless, hope where we feel hopeless, and acceptance when we feel rejected. May our longing for change prompt us to look toward Jesus as we round the corner of our journey through Luke, and

42

may this spirit prompt us to open ourselves to God and all that He offers through His Son, Jesus.

The characters in the story from Luke 13 seem a lot like us. At times, they struggled, even with Jesus right beside them. He walked, ate, and related to them in humanlike fashion, but His supernatural aura kept them continually curious. They hoped He was The Promised One. In this passage, they questioned Him. The way Jesus answered them was interesting, even paradoxical. Many of the things they had always considered sin, like the healing of a disabled woman on the Sabbath, He proclaimed were not. At the same time, He rebuked them for other things like not bearing spiritual fruit—love, joy, peace, patience, kindness, goodness, faithfulness, gentleness, and self-control. He wanted them to live lives of self-sacrifice filled with these fruits and, as He explained, walk through the narrow door of life rather than the broad, easy one.

When He said in Matthew 20:16, "So the last will be first, and the first last," His words became even more challenging. Whether He was rebuking or encouraging them, He always focused on a relationship with Him rather than the rules or religion of the day.

Some of us fight the pull to check off spiritual boxes—like going to church or attending Bible studies or taking mission trips—in an attempt to gain God's favor and other people's approval. We might even have thought at times, *If I do this for God, then God will do that for me.* But if Christianity is about a relationship, then this mindset is flawed. A healthy relationship is built on both people asking *what can I give?* rather than *what can I get?* Jesus continues to invite the people, and us, into relationship with Him.

This God that they had always seen as distant was now inviting them to admit their sin and come close to Him. He reminded them that obedience was not only following a list of laws but also responding to the One who loved them beyond imagination.

Chapter 13 closes on such a sweet note. With a spirit of sadness, Jesus leaned in and spoke to the people, and to the entire city of Jerusalem, saying His heart longed to nestle them into the warmth of His presence and protection, much like a hen gathers her frail and helpless chicks. In the midst of a conflicted state of humanity, He simply loved them. In the midst of our struggles and sin, He also loves us.

Repentance is about returning to Him with a desire to change and receiving His forgiveness, love, and acceptance. It's about offering our lives to Him, over and over and over again. Repentance is reconnecting with God in an attitude of humility and belief in Him as our Savior. The Bible says in Romans 2:4, "God's kindness is meant to lead you to repentance." It's really about coming back under His protective wing.

No matter where we are in our journey with God, may we always feel we are at the halfway point, that we are somewhere between the garden of Eden and eternity.

While we will not see the completion of this story until He returns, may our journey stir hope for what is to come and a realization of our need for Jesus, the One who completes us. Let's find comfort as we nestle beneath His wings of love and protection.

Process
1. In what ways do you feel insecure today?
2. Identify a part of your life that feels peaceful as well as one that feels difficult. Ask God to help you live with this difficulty by feeling His presence.
3. In your life, when have you felt closest to God?

Prayer

Heavenly Father, when everything feels meaningless, remind me of Your purposes for my life. When I feel hopeless, remind me that You are my anchor. When rejection inevitably comes, give me the ability to see my value through Your eyes.

Promise

"Come to me, all who labor and are heavy laden, and I will give you rest." (Matthew 11:28)

Luke 14—Savor

Blessed is everyone who will eat bread in the kingdom of God!

—Luke 14:15

Have you ever met a friend for dinner only for that friend to say, "I'm not eating tonight, but you go ahead." While this might not bother some people, it might ruin the meal for others. For many of us, fully enjoying a meal is only possible when it is shared. "Mmmmm. This is delicious! It's seasoned just right!" Or, "This reminds me of the wine we once had on that trip." Or, "This steak is cooked to perfection!" My husband and I enjoy tasting the first bite of our meal at the same moment. We watch each other's expressions, and sometimes no words are needed as we nod and grin. Eating together is just better than eating alone!

Jesus often sat and ate with people as He connected with them. We can only imagine the privilege of sharing a meal with Him while having meaningful conversation. Think of the type of evening where you want to linger for hours and enjoy the company of friends. Jesus did this. He took His time talking with and listening to anyone with whom He shared a meal. Even in His final days on earth, Jesus used His time with the disciples during their last supper together to share spiritual truths. The table seemed to mean a great deal to Jesus. Let's dig deeper into Luke for the significance regarding the table at which Jesus sat.

Luke 14 invites us to observe three banquets. At the first banquet, Jesus challenged His listeners to leave the place of honor at the table unoccupied. He encouraged them to find a seat at the foot of the table rather than at the head. He told them, "For everyone who exalts himself will be humbled, and he who humbles himself will be exalted" (v. 11). At the second banquet, He instructed them to invite guests who could not repay the favor. "Invite the poor, the crippled, the lame, the blind," Jesus said (v. 13). He seemed to be encouraging them to focus on giving to people without expecting anything in return. What a beautiful picture of grace! At the third banquet, the invited guests didn't show up. The host instructed his servants to go out into the streets and invite the poor, the crippled, the lame, and the blind. Note that Jesus used these four identical descriptive words in two different stories, reiterating His point.

As we have moved through the book of Luke, we've learned about a consistent characteristic of Jesus: He never taught a truth that He didn't demonstrate in His own life. He always walked His talk.

Some of us might look at these stories, see a set of rules, and think, *If Jesus did this, I should too.* Or, *He commanded us to reach out to marginalized people, and if we do this, then we will be blessed.* While we likely will be blessed in a number of ways if we do what Jesus instructs, there is another point to consider. Let's look at these stories from a different angle. Instead of putting ourselves in the role of the host, let's imagine that we are the invited guests and Jesus is our host. He welcomes us despite our imperfections and brokenness, and we are invited to feast at the table with Him. As we receive acceptance at His table, we in turn have the freedom to welcome others to ours. He loves us so we can love others. First John 4:19 says, "We love because he first loved us."

No matter who we are or what we've done, Jesus invites us to feast upon and savor life with Him. Metaphorically speaking, we are all poor, crippled, lame, and blind, and we are not worthy to be invited to His table. But Jesus came to earth, making communion with God possible. Isaiah 55:1 says,

> Come, everyone who thirsts,
>   come to the waters;
> and he who has no money,
>   come, buy and eat!
> Come, buy wine and milk
>   without money and without price.

Jesus calls to us, inviting us to come to Him, despite our shortcomings and imperfections. What qualifies us to be invited to feast with Jesus? Absolutely nothing. Only because of His grace are we invited, even chosen, to sit beside Him at the table.

Savor means to taste and enjoy completely. When we sit around the table this Christmas savoring food, friends, and family, may we be reminded that "He brought me to the banqueting house, and his banner over me was love" (Song of Solomon 2:4). As we realize that Jesus welcomes us just as we are, let us in turn welcome others. May we be always grateful for God's grace and love, and may we wholeheartedly accept the invitation to feast with Him.

Process
1. Do you see God as a heavy-handed taskmaster or as a friend inviting you to a lovely dinner party?

2. In what areas do you feel like you must perform in order to please God?
3. Ask God for a new way to receive His grace today.

Prayer

Only You, Jesus, qualify me to join the feast with Your Father. It is because of Your grace that I am invited, even chosen, to sit beside You at the table. Even on my worst day, when I am the least deserving child, You welcome me. Thank You.

Promise

"I will come in to him and eat with him, and he with me."
(Revelation 3:20)

Luke 15—Return

Just so, I tell you, there will be more joy in heaven over one sinner who repents than over ninety-nine righteous persons who need no repentance.

—Luke 15:7

With my terrible sense of direction, I can easily get off course. I can drive for miles and miles without realizing I'm headed in the wrong direction. Once, after filling up with gas, I returned to the interstate and drove north when I should have driven south. It was not until I saw an exit sign for a major city that I realized what I had done. I said aloud to the empty car, "How did I do this? I must be crazy!" I didn't even know I was lost.

In chapter 15, Luke described a time when many types of people gathered around Jesus. Verse 1 says that on this particular day, the tax collectors and sinners were "drawing near to hear Him." The Pharisees and scribes looked on, criticizing Jesus and thinking highly of themselves. They thought they were living blameless, faultless, righteous lives. In their opinion, Jesus should not have been spending time with sinners, much less sharing a meal with them! They wondered why the Son of God would associate with such lowly, disgusting people.

Jesus, of course, disagreed. It was time, once again, to explain Himself through parables. In fact, this particular point was so important to Him that He told three stories, back to back, about lost things.

In the first narrative, we find ourselves in the middle of a pasture, surrounded by one hundred sheep that are led by a shepherd who realizes one of them has been lost. He cared deeply enough to leave the ninety-nine, hoping to find the one lost lamb. Upon recovering the adventurous lost sheep, he rejoiced greatly. Jesus then explained that this one lost lamb can be compared to one lost sinner. He said, "There will be more joy in heaven over one sinner who repents than over ninety-nine righteous persons who need no repentance" (v. 7).

Next, we are escorted into a dimly lit house, as Jesus told the story of a woman who had lost one of her ten coins. She brightened the rooms and carefully searched her house, much like you or I might when we lose a credit card or our phone. Sweeping the floors, she searched everywhere until she found her treasured coin. And when she found it, she rejoiced! Similarly, just as this one small coin held great value to the woman, one lost sinner holds great value in the eyes of God.

The third narrative is powerful and compelling and has an unexpected ending. We move from a lost animal and a lost coin to a lost person.

This story involves a young man, one who became lost in a different way. This younger son requested an early inheritance from his father. His father agreed, and a few days later, the son packed his belongings and his inheritance and moved away. After squandering all his money, he was forced to get a job feeding pigs in order to stay alive. Hungry enough to eat the pigs' food, he suddenly realized he could return home, admit what he had done, and ask to be hired as his father's servant. But instead, upon his homecoming, he found that his dad was not angry; in fact, his father had been waiting, looking, and hoping for his son to return. The two reunited with a warm embrace. Regardless of what the son had done, the father accepted him without judgment. Although the young man might have expected rejection, there was no discord, anger, or conflict—only grace and acceptance. Rejoicing that the lost has been found, the father reminded him that he always had a place at home, just because he was his son. The hurting son deserved nothing, but his loving father gave him everything.

Some may see the sheep, the coin, and the son in these stories representing a person who accepts Christ for the first time. Certainly, there is great rejoicing and celebration for those who accept Jesus as their Savior. But what about the person who has been a Christian for a long time? Much of the time, we believe that we know what is best and we attempt to selfishly control our circumstances. But going our own way without trusting God can lead us to a place of being lost, alone, confused, even hopeless.

No matter how often we go our own way and get lost, Jesus is always there to take us back. When the shepherd found the lost sheep, he laid it on his shoulders as he rejoiced (vv. 5–6). When the woman realized she had lost a treasure, she diligently sought the lost coin (v. 8). And when the father of the lost boy saw him, he felt compassion for him and ran to embrace him and kiss him (v. 20).

Every day, no matter how distant God might seem, He seeks us. Remembering His grace, we can return to Him, where He will be waiting for us with love and acceptance. He holds us, rejoices over us, embraces us, and reminds us that we always have a place with Him.

The sheep seem to always have a prominent role in the manger scene at Christmas. From Christmas cards to store-front windows, sheep are everywhere. This Christmas when we see these sheep, may we be reminded that when we are lost, Jesus still loves us and invites us to return to Him. May we never forget that He is always waiting for us, hoping we will return.

Process

1. Does repentance make you feel shame, or does it bring you back to Jesus?
2. How can you draw near to God today?
3. Thank Jesus that He still loves you, no matter what, as you repent and return to Him.

Prayer

No matter how often I lose my way, Jesus, You always welcome me back into a relationship with You. Your unconditional love astonishes me. No matter how badly I've failed, no matter how far I've strayed, You still desire to be close to me. This almost seems too good to be true.

Promise

"Consequently, he is able to save to the uttermost those who draw near to God through him, since he always lives to make intercession for them." (Hebrews 7:25)

Luke 16—Relinquish

One who is faithful in a very little is also faithful in much.

—Luke 16:10

Have you ever tried to pry a toy from the hand of a toddler? Like a small child, we sometimes have a propensity to grasp tightly something we love until our knuckles turn white. The picture of giving over something you deeply care about is the theme of today's reading in Luke 16. We find a shorter chapter that is on point concerning the theme of relinquishment. *Relinquish* means to let go of, release, give over control, or stop holding on to. Both parables found in this chapter talk about riches and financial security. The first story tells of a rich man whose property manager wasted his money. As a result, the rich man told him that he was about to be fired. In response, the manager reached out to all the people who owed the rich man money and cut their debt nearly in half. His goal was to make friends so that he would have people to take him in when he was without work. Sometimes, Jesus let the parable speak for itself, but this time He clearly stated the four lessons to be learned: invest your resources creatively to build and grow relationships (v. 9); if you are faithful in little, you will be faithful in much (v. 10); if you can't be trusted with worldly wealth, who would trust you with the true riches of heaven (v. 12)? And finally, Jesus closed by saying, "You cannot serve God and money" (v. 13).

Jesus drove the principle of relinquishment home as He told another parable on the subject of wealth. We are introduced to another rich man who refused to help a poor man covered with sores who lay right outside his gate, longing for leftovers from his table. The two men eventually died; the needy man arrived in heaven and the rich man in hell. In torment and fear, the rich man begged Abraham to return to earth and warn his five brothers to repent of their sins and turn to God so they would not end up like him. Clearly, Jesus was teaching His followers to love God more than money and possessions.

In an effort to further understand these parables, allow me to tell a tale of two crafty young teenagers who broke into a clothing store in the middle of the night in order to play a mischievous and destructive prank. The boys hacked into the store's computer system and assigned new, much lower prices to every item. Careful to leave no evidence behind, they then left the store and waited for it to open. When it did, confusion and turmoil reigned.

The question to consider is this: How have we swapped the price tags for things of this world? We have placed high value on things that don't really matter to God, and we have placed low value on things that matter greatly to Him. We seem to have it backwards, according to Jesus's teaching. So what exactly matters to God? Jesus tells us not to look at things that are seen but rather at things that are unseen (2 Corinthians 4:18). Most of the time, material wealth is easy to see. Faith, hope, and love—which are valued by God—are harder for us to see. Again, Jesus explained in verse 13, "No servant can serve two masters, for either he will hate the one and love the other, or he will be devoted to the one and despise the other. You cannot serve God and money."

I've heard this spiritual value system described as "God's economy." We are pulled toward comfort, ease, and a life of security by striving to obtain material things. We work hard and put much effort toward these goals—having a good job, a nice home, and a new car—when, in reality, God is more concerned with the condition of our hearts.

When Jesus talked about material possessions, He turned to the theme of stewardship. *Stewardship* means "utilizing and managing all resources God provides for the glory of God and the betterment of His creation" (Holman Bible Dictionary). In other words, when we acknowledge that all we have belongs to God, we are free to use what we have been given to benefit others as we glorify Him. We have the opportunity to live our lives for Him, valuing what He values—the unseen rather than the seen.

In light of what we are learning, these parables about letting go of earthly things are given to us by a Father who loves us and cares for us and who rejoices in our joy and hurts when we hurt. He created us to be complete in Him alone. He knows that when we look for security and happiness in possessions, we will ultimately be disappointed. The temporary things of the world were never meant to satisfy our deepest needs. They only offer false security. But Jesus offers us true security in Him. He offers faith, hope, and love. He offers abundant life. John 10:10 says, "I came that they may have life and have it abundantly."

What about us? Are we regularly feeling let down or disappointed? What causes pain or leaves us feeling empty? Sometimes Christmas can be a time of focusing too much on material things as well as looking to people for fulfillment. Let's consider realigning the things in which we place our security by reassigning value and relinquishing the things and relationships of this world. Let's allow God, who cares deeply about us, to fill us with the completion He offers through His Son, Jesus.

Process

1. What things in your life do you grasp tightly out of fear or control?
2. What would the idea of relinquishment look like to you in these areas?
3. Pray and ask God to help you let go of these things and give Him control, realizing that He loves you and has a perfect plan for you.

Prayer

Dear God, I continue to struggle when I search for security and happiness in the people and things of this world. Thank You for offering me true security, faith, hope, and love when I bond with You. You offer abundant life beyond anything I can imagine. May I let go of the things that are not meant to satisfy me and cling to You, my Rock.

Promise

"From the Lord you will receive the inheritance as your reward." (Colossians 3:24)

Luke 17—Sacrifice

Whoever seeks to preserve his life will lose it, but whoever loses his life will keep it.

—Luke 17:33

A few years ago, a tornado came through Tuscaloosa in our home state of Alabama. We heard a story of a twenty-one-year-old scholar athlete who held up a concrete wall long enough for his girlfriend to make it to safety. But in the end, the wall fell on him, killing him. In another example of self-sacrifice, a young man who graduated from a local high school and went on to serve our country as a soldier in the Middle East was killed by a roadside bomb. While so many people in our community mourned his death, we all were reminded of John 15:13, which says, "Greater love has no one than this, that someone lay down his life for his friends." And what about Todd Beamer, the hero on Flight 93 that fateful day on September 11, 2001? He, along with several other passengers, sacrificed their lives in an attempt to thwart the terrorists' plot to crash their plane into the US Capitol or the White House. Only moments before the plane went down, he led them in the Lord's Prayer, some of the last words the passengers ever heard.

More recently, we saw incredible self-sacrifice from healthcare workers around the world who risked their lives to save others from the deadly COVID-19 virus.

At this point in the book of Luke, the story shifts. Jesus and His disciples faced trying times, and His teachings grew more challenging. The plot builds as it leads to Jesus facing the ultimate sacrifice on our behalf.

Sacrifice is defined as an act of giving up something valued for the sake of something else regarded as more important or worthy. Sacrifice is difficult. Spiritual sacrifice is impossible when living apart from God. Everything within us seems to pull us toward self-satisfaction. A life filled with sacrifices, whether small or large, does not come naturally. But at the same time, when we hear stories of those who have given their lives for something or someone else, we are compelled to make sacrifices of our own.

The strange and curious thing about stories of sacrifice is that they are both tragic and beautiful, heart-wrenching and redemptive, distressing and hopeful. Deep grief over a lost life is followed by joy and gratitude for lives saved. This is the theme of Jesus's life. He was to die in order to save us. He regularly hinted at His future to those around Him, often confusing them. Even His twelve disciples couldn't understand what was coming. He encouraged forgiveness and repentance as He saw His time on earth coming to an end (v. 4), and He taught His followers how to walk by faith, knowing it would carry them forward when He was gone (v. 6).

Repentance, faith, humility, and gratitude are all themes in this chapter. Jesus highlighted these as important characteristics for those who wished to follow Him. Some call it the backwards life. Living a life of servitude and sacrifice is counterintuitive to our human nature. We naturally tend toward self-preservation and self-satisfaction. But let's look at an example of these characteristics. Beginning in verse 11, Jesus's journey toward Jerusalem continued, and He entered a village between Galilee and

Samaria. Ten people infected with leprosy cried out to Him to show them mercy.

Jesus told them to go show themselves to the priests, and as they walked to the temple to do so, they were healed. Only one of the ten then returned to thank Jesus for what He had done, "praising God with a loud voice" (v. 15). The other nine did not return. Are we like the one leper who returned in gratitude, or do we go on our way, failing to thank God for His blessings?

Most of us want our lives to display characteristics of self-sacrifice and serving others, but most of us don't naturally follow this path. Instead, we seek lives of ease and comfort and even self-absorption. But while a life of sacrifice can seem difficult and unpleasant, it is also fulfilling and beautiful. Have you ever experienced deep satisfaction when God gave you the strength to put someone else's needs before yours? It's rewarding beyond measure. So how can we live out God's instructions to repent and have faith, humility, and gratitude? Saturate ourselves in God's grace. Jesus gave us the most vivid representation of a life of self-sacrifice. He came and presented Himself as the ultimate sacrifice. Philippians 2:6–8 says, Jesus "who, though he was in the form of God, did not count equality with God a thing to be grasped, but emptied himself, by taking the form of a servant, being born in the likeness of men. And being found in human form, he humbled himself by becoming obedient to the point of death, even death on a cross."

The surprising result of living a sacrificial life is the satisfaction and joy that always follows. God's grace pouring through His children is overwhelming and glorious. When God sent His Son to earth, He provided a way to Himself. We were lost and then found. We were helpless and then saved. We were nothing and then, if we accept Him, we are everything. We are children of God. Serving others comes naturally when we understand our need and God's provision. This Christmas may we remember the reason for His coming and never fail to return to Him in grateful praise.

Process
1. What do the words *repentance, faith, humility,* and *gratitude* mean to you?
2. How do you see God giving you grace in your life today?
3. How can you extend this grace to someone else?

Prayer
Dear God, when You sent Your Son, Jesus Christ, to earth, You provided a way for me, covered in His righteousness, to come to You. I was lost and then found. I was helpless and then saved. I had nothing, and when I continue to accept You, I have everything. Thank You, Father, that I am Your beloved child.

Promise
"It is more blessed to give than to receive." (Acts 20:35)

Luke 18—See

*And immediately he recovered his sight and followed
him, glorifying God. And all the people, when they saw
it, gave praise to God.*

—Luke 18:43

Children see things differently than adults. They see with sim-
plicity. They see with innocence. They see with purity. Christmas
through the eyes of a child is magical. I remember as a little girl
hardly being able to fall asleep on Christmas Eve. It was not only
about the gifts to be opened but also about the decorations, the
food, our family, and celebrating the birth of Jesus. There was no
better feeling than lining up with my siblings, youngest first, then
tiptoeing in to find the tree lit, the stockings full, and the cookies
we had left for Santa Claus gone. It was a feast for the eyes!

In Luke 18, children are brought to the forefront of Jesus's ministry. One day some parents brought their young children to Jesus
so He would touch them (v. 15). It seems these parents felt that if
Jesus simply placed His hands on their children, they would be
blessed. But when the disciples saw this happening, they scolded
them. The disciples must have thought this was a waste of Jesus's
time, or maybe they thought spending time with children was
beneath Him.

But Jesus surprised them. He responded by calling the children to Himself. "Let the children come to me, and do not hinder
them, for to such belongs the kingdom of God" (v. 16). Jesus went

on to further His point in verse 17 when He said, "Whoever does not receive the kingdom of God like a child shall not enter it." The term *kingdom of God* is defined as "the spiritual realm over which God reigns as king, or the fulfillment on Earth of God's will" (Britannica). Jesus was saying that unless we receive and accept God's reign over earth's spiritual realm like a child—humbly, innocently, completely—we will never be allowed to become a part of it. Like a child fully trusts his or her parents, we fully trust our God. We truly see Him as our protector, our provider, and our Father. We see Him, like a child might see his earthly father, as our everything.

In Luke 18, Jesus took His disciples aside to talk about His impending death. For the third time in Luke, He predicted His death and resurrection by reminding them of the prophets' words from Psalms, Isaiah, and Zechariah. And how did His disciples react? They didn't understand. The significance of His words was hidden from them (v. 34), and they couldn't grasp what He was saying. Their eyes had not yet been opened to comprehend what was coming. Let's think about our lives. Is God trying to tell us something that we can't or won't receive? Is He trying to guide us down a path that we have not chosen? Let's open our eyes and ears in faith and experience Him as He leads us toward the future He wants for us.

Finally in chapter 18, Luke tells us a story about Jesus and a crowd of people on their way to Jericho. As they approached the city, a man shouted, "Jesus, Son of David, have mercy on me!" (v. 38). The people told the man to be quiet, but he only yelled louder. When Jesus heard the shouting, He ordered the man to be brought to Him and asked the man what he wanted. "Lord, let me recover my sight" (v. 41). Jesus replied, "Recover your sight;

your faith has made you well" (v. 42). The blind man expressed his need, believed Jesus could cure him, and because of his faith, was instantly healed.

This story reveals truth on both a physical and spiritual level. Jesus cured the man physically, healing his blindness. We're told in verse 43 that after the man was healed, he followed Jesus, praising God. And then we're told that all who saw the miracle healing praised God too. The very people who had told the blind man to be quiet were now praising God that Jesus had stopped to take the time to cure him. It seems Jesus took the opportunity to heal on a physical level, knowing He would in turn be making an impact on a spiritual level. The people needed to see a miracle in order to also see Jesus for who He really was—the Messiah.

Today, let's consider our focus. What do we see when we look around? Do we see lights and gifts and decorations? Or do we see God's love for us in the person of His Son, Jesus? Let's ask Him to help us see Jesus through the eyes of a child: simply, innocently, and with pure trust. Wide-eyed like a child on Christmas morning, may we look to Him to guide and direct us through this festive season, as well as through life.

May we see Jesus as our healer, our Savior, and most of all, our God.

Process

1. Why does it seem so easy to focus on the things around us rather than fixing our eyes on Jesus?
2. What does faith have to do with seeing and trusting God?
3. What is one thing you know to be true about God that might help you more fully trust Him?

Prayer

Open my eyes with excitement and expectation like a child on Christmas morning. May I look to You to guide and direct me through this festive season, as well as through life. May I see You as my healer, my Savior, and most of all, my God.

Promise

"The LORD opens the eyes of the blind." (Psalm 146:8)

Luke 19—Enter

Blessed is the King who comes in the name of the Lord!
Peace in heaven and glory in the highest!

—Luke 19:38

Luke 19 finds Jesus entering and making His way through the town of Jericho, once again surrounded by many people. We're introduced to a man named Zacchaeus, the region's chief tax collector who was quite wealthy. The people called him a sinner because he had cheated many out of their money. Like the others in Jericho, Zacchaeus was scrambling to see Jesus. The scene may have been like a Christmas parade where layers of people line the streets to see the main attraction. But because of his height, he couldn't see over the people in front of him to get a glimpse of this religious figure who had come to town. So what did Zacchaeus do? He climbed a tree beside the road that Jesus was expected to travel. As Jesus passed by, He looked up at Zacchaeus and called him by name. "Zacchaeus, hurry and come down, for I must stay at your house today" (v. 5). Imagine how Zacchaeus must have felt, singled out of the crowd by this important person. We're told he felt great excitement and joy as he climbed down the tree and took Jesus to his house.

The next part of the story is a bit of a mystery. We're not told what Jesus said to Zacchaeus while they spent time together in his home, but we know the conversation must have been both meaningful and powerful. However, we do know how Zacchaeus responded. He said, "Behold, Lord, the half of my goods I give to the poor. And if I have defrauded anyone of anything, I restore it fourfold" (v. 8). What could Jesus have said to generate such a change of heart in this dishonest man? Or could it have been the simple fact that Jesus was willing to enter Zacchaeus's house despite his awful reputation? Whatever happened behind those doors, and whatever Jesus might have said, the encounter ended with Jesus announcing, "Today salvation has come to this house" (v. 9). The change in Zacchaeus came after he opened himself to Jesus with a willingness to change. Are we open to what Jesus is trying to tell us? Have we, like Zacchaeus, welcomed Him in? He tells us in Revelation 3:20, "I stand at the door and knock. If anyone hears my voice and opens the door, I will come in to him and eat with him, and he with me." He is waiting for us to open the door to Him so He can do miraculous things in our lives as well.

Luke 19 moves forward to a different kind of entry: a triumphant entry. After Jesus left Jericho and approached Jerusalem, He sent two disciples ahead to bring Him a young donkey, a colt that no one had ever ridden. This is how Jesus chose to enter the Holy City—the site of His upcoming death and resurrection— riding on a donkey.

This simple act, predicted in Zechariah, speaks to Jesus's humility. This King, this Savior, this Messiah could have chosen a grand entrance, one with much fanfare and celebration, but that was not in keeping with God's plan. Instead, much like the humble surroundings into which He was born, He humbly rode a donkey covered with the disciples' garments on a road covered with the crowd's garments. The people erupted into shouting and singing as He passed: "Blessed is the King who comes in the name of the Lord! Peace in heaven, and glory in the highest!" (v. 38).

The air must have been filled with a palpable excitement as the people watched Him pass.

Have you ever received a Christmas gift and thought you knew what was hidden inside? I remember receiving a plain white envelope from my husband one Christmas morning. I had no idea what it held, but I guessed a gift certificate of some sort or maybe tickets to a play or musical event. I would have been thrilled with any of these gifts. But I was so wrong, and what I found inside that envelope took me by surprise. My husband had planned a trip to Europe—somewhere I had never been but always hoped to go. That plain envelope hid something so surprising, so special, and to me, so overwhelming. I never would have imagined the magnitude of the gift by looking at the envelope.

Similarly, Jesus did not fulfill the expectations many people had for their king. By earthly standards He was plain, and they wanted a king that looked the part, one surrounded by luxury and fanfare. But Jesus was the son of a carpenter, born in a stable, and riding a donkey into Jerusalem. In Zechariah 9:9 we're told,

> Behold, your king is coming to you;
>   righteous and having salvation is he,
> humble and mounted on a donkey,
>   on a colt, the foal of a donkey.

Some of the people couldn't see past Jesus's humble appearance. They couldn't accept Him as their king. This made Jesus weep (v. 41). We're told in verse 37 that at this point in Jesus's life and ministry, the priests, teachers, and other leaders began planning to kill Him. They were unable to recognize Him for who He really was. They were jealous of and threatened by His influence over the people.

Do we recognize Jesus for who He was and is—God's Son? Have we invited Him into our lives like Zacchaeus invited Jesus into his home? Have we listened to His words, opened our hearts to Him, and let Him change us? Let's ask Him to transform us. We have only to open the door and allow Him to enter, and He will begin to accomplish things through us and for us that we could never have imagined.

Process
1. In what way do you need to be saved by God today?
2. Name three traits of God for which you can be thankful.
3. Are there any practical ways you can invite God into your life on a daily basis?

Prayer
Jesus, may I not just listen to Your words, but may I allow Your Spirit to open my heart. I ask You to transform me. By Your Spirit, may I open the door, allowing You to enter. Help me to trust that You will begin to accomplish things through me and for me that I could never have imagined or accomplished on my own.

Promise
"For the Son of Man came to seek and to save the lost." (Luke 19:10)

Luke 20—Elevate

Sit at my right hand,
until I make your enemies your footstool.

—Luke 20:42–43

Our society seems to have become more opinionated and divided in recent years. With the constant barrage of information flowing across so many media channels, we hear it all. We can watch two news outlets cover the same event, only to have it feel like two different stories. And the fact-checkers have an agenda as well. It seems the only way to find the truth is to listen to all sides of an issue and then, using that information coupled with our discernment, decide what or whom to believe. It can be exhausting.

The religious leaders watching Jesus had become combative. They had grown obsessed with finding a way to trick Jesus into saying something that would land Him in trouble with the religious and political leaders of the day. In Luke 20, Jesus's enemies challenged Him. Verse 2 tells us the leading priests, the teachers of religious law, and the elders demanded, "Tell us by what authority you do these things, or who it is that gave you this authority." Instead of engaging in an argument, Jesus answered them with a question. He asked them where they believed John the Baptist received his authority.

When they refused to answer His question, He in turn wouldn't directly answer theirs. Instead, He told them a story, a parable about a group of evil tenant farmers turned murderers. After He finished telling the story, the religious leaders realized that the evil farmers in His story represented them. He had turned the tables on their evil intentions to trick Him. He had silenced them. They desperately wanted to arrest Jesus, but they were afraid of the people's reaction (v. 19).

Again in Luke 20 the religious leaders attempted to trick Jesus. This time they sent spies to try to get Jesus to say something that would warrant His arrest (v. 20). Their strategy began with flattery. "Teacher, we know that you speak and teach rightly, and show no partiality, but truly teach the way of God" (v. 21). They then asked Him if it was necessary to pay taxes to the government, hoping to trap Him when He contradicted Caesar, the Roman emperor. He recognized their evil ploy, and in His wisdom, He rose above their evil intentions by calmly giving them a simple answer. Pointing out that Caesar's picture was on the Roman coin, Jesus replied, "Then render to Caesar the things that are Caesar's, and to God the things that are God's" (v. 25). Once again, amazed, His enemies were silenced as they failed to trap Him with their questions.

For a third time in this chapter, Luke tells us about another group of religious leaders who tried to stump Jesus with what they thought was an unanswerable question. They presented a scenario where a woman married the oldest of seven brothers. He died, leaving her a childless widow. They go on to explain that the widow married the next oldest brother, as their custom required, but he died too. She then married every one of the brothers, seven in all, and every one of them eventually died, leaving her with no children. Finally, they said, the woman died as well. Then came the question they hoped would entrap Jesus: "In the resurrection, therefore, whose wife will the woman be? For the seven had her as wife" (v. 33). Jesus's reply was immediate. "The sons of this age marry and are given in marriage" (v. 34). After He further explained that the Lord was the God of the living, some of His enemies responded, "Teacher, you have spoken well" (v. 39). Once again, His enemies were silenced.

Now it was Jesus's turn to ask an unanswerable question. "How can they say that the Christ is David's son?" (v. 41). He added in verse 44, "David thus calls him Lord, so how is he his son?" Before they could come up with an answer, Jesus turned to the people surrounding Him and continued to teach. It was as if He didn't want or expect the religious leaders to answer His question; instead, He wanted to show them that He was not intimidated by their questions. He simply made His point by asking a question to which they had no answer. He, once again, elevated Himself above His enemies' attacks.

Have we elevated ourselves above the swirl of opinions surrounding us on a daily basis? Are we able to sift through the mounds of information we constantly encounter?

And what about the overload of activities during the Christmas season? Let's think about what really matters, at Christmas or any other time of year. Jesus. He is what matters. His birth, His life, His death and resurrection. It's time to more intentionally set our focus on Him and allow His words to elevate us above the noise. Let's draw near to Him these last few days leading up to the celebration of His birth and simplify our Christmas. May we turn down the volume of the distractions around us in order to more clearly hear Jesus's message of love.

Process
1. Do you seek being right over being respectful?
2. How can we see Jesus as full of grace and full of truth?

3. Are there any sources from which you could disconnect in order to prevent disruption within?

Prayer

Lord, may I always see afresh Your birth, Your life, Your death, and Your resurrection. Help me to more intentionally set my focus on You and allow Your words to elevate me above the distractions that swirl around me.

Promise

"GOD, the Lord, is my strength;
  he makes my feet like the deer's;
  he makes me tread on my high places." (Habakkuk 3:19)

Luke 21—Prepare

And then they will see the Son of Man coming in a
cloud with power and great glory.

—Luke 21:27

Luke 21 opens with a simple but powerful story, again about humility and sacrifice. On this particular day in the temple, Jesus watched as wealthy people dropped gifts in the collection box. Then a poor widow dropped in two coins—small Jewish copper coins, worth very little. Jesus took the opportunity to reveal a truth based on the woman's actions. He said in verse 3, "This poor widow has put in more than all of them." He went on to explain that the wealthy people had given a small part of their surplus, but she had given everything she had.

For most of us, it's easy to give out of excess, but Jesus wants us, like the widow, to trust Him enough to give when we feel we have no excess. Christmastime might be the perfect opportunity to live out this truth. Some years, we might feel we barely have the resources to provide Christmas for our own family and loved ones. How could we possibly give to someone in need if we have no surplus? Let's revisit the widow's actions. Verse 4 says, "She out of her poverty put in all she had to live on." This woman took the little money that she had—and likely needed to survive— and sacrificially gave it away. Clearly, she trusted God to provide for her future needs. Do we trust God like that? Do we believe that He will take care of us when we've come to the end of our resources? Paul says in Philippians 4:19, "And my God will supply every need of yours according to his riches in glory in Christ Jesus."

In the remainder of this chapter, Luke tells us that Jesus taught daily in the temple, and crowds gathered early each morning to hear Him. As the end of His ministry and life drew near, Jesus turned His teachings toward the future. In Luke 21, Jesus walked His followers through the signs that will take place before the end of days. It might be difficult for some of us to hear His words and apply them to our lives, but let's look at His teachings with open hearts and minds and prayerfully discover how to properly process these prophetic truths.

Jesus foretold the future when He overheard His disciples talking about the majestic stonework and memorial decorations on the temple walls. Jesus interjected, "The days will come when there will not be left here one stone upon another that will not be thrown down" (v. 6). According to Scripture, Jesus paralleled the coming destruction of the temple—which occurred in AD 70 when the Romans took Jerusalem and burned it—with His future return to earth, or His second coming. The disciples asked when all this would happen, and Jesus responded by naming a number of things that would take place prior to the end. Let's take a look at the signs, in chronological order, that Jesus explained would occur before the end of time:

- Persecution of Jesus's followers will take place. (v. 12)
- Families and friends will betray one another. (v. 16)
- Jesus's followers will be hated. (v. 17)
- Many will come in His name, claiming to be the Messiah and saying the end has come. (v. 8)
- Wars and insurrections will occur. (v. 9)

- Earthquakes, famines, and plagues will cover many lands. (v. 11)
- Strange signs will appear in the sun, moon, and stars. (v. 25)
- Nations will be in turmoil, perplexed by the roaring seas and the waves. (v. 25)
- People will be terrified; "the powers of the heavens will be shaken." (v. 26)
- Everyone "will see the Son of Man coming in a cloud with power and great glory." (v. 27)

After Jesus explained these coming events to His disciples, He went on to help them understand how to prepare for the future by giving them two clear instructions. First, in verse 34, He warned them to watch themselves by not letting their hearts become weighed down with the cares of this life. Second, in verse 36, He told them to keep alert and pray for strength.

So we have these unsettling predictions and compelling instructions laid out before us. Jesus provided a beautiful promise to His followers in verses 13–15. In the midst of the trying times to come, He told us that this will be our opportunity to tell people about Him. He told us not to worry because He said, "I will give you a mouth and wisdom, which none of your adversaries will be able to withstand or contradict." Much like Jesus was able to wisely silence His enemies throughout His ministry on earth, He promised we will be able to do the same. How reassuring to know that although difficult times are ahead, He will provide the tools we need to not only survive but also be a beacon of light for Him.

As heavy as this chapter might feel, a parallel unfolds that can be applied to us this Christmas. The final week of Jesus's life on earth—the week of Passover—had come. He knew what the future held. He surely felt a sense of urgency, a need to make the most of His time. And what did He do? He gave the few free days He had remaining to the people—teaching, warning, and encouraging them. What a perfect example for us these last few days before Christmas as we prepare for the celebration of His birth. As Jesus instructed, let's keep alert and pray. We have three days left before Christmas. Let us join with those around us as we reflect on the person of Jesus by looking back at His life and looking forward to His birth. May we intentionally share Christ's love with others during this sacred season.

Process

1. What is unsettling for you today?
2. Can you find a promise in God's Word that brings peace?
3. Ask God to prepare a place in your heart to receive Him this Christmas.

Prayer

Jesus, how reassuring to know that, although difficult times are ahead, You will provide all that I need to not only survive but also be a beacon of light for You. Please show me that You are near. I'm looking today for Your light on my path.

Promise

"Now when these things begin to take place, straighten up and raise your heads, because your redemption is drawing near." (Luke 21:28)

Luke 22—Wrestle

Father, if you are willing, remove this cup from me.
Nevertheless, not my will, but yours, be done.

—Luke 22:42

Have you ever dreaded something difficult? The results of a medical test? A looming legal matter? News of your company's restructuring? The day of reckoning will inevitably arrive, but the apprehension sometimes proves almost as unbearable as the day itself. The anticipation can be misery.

The end of Jesus's life was at hand, and He knew it. In Luke 22, He moved toward His crucifixion with purpose, continuing to make the most of every opportunity to love those around Him while facing an agonizing death. He gathered His disciples for the Passover meal, their last supper together, and talked with them about the many things that were to come. He spoke about a new covenant between God and His people, sealed with His own blood as a sacrifice for them. He spoke about the disciple who would betray Him. He challenged them to be servant-leaders and promised they would one day sit on thrones.

After this Last Supper, Jesus went with His disciples to the Mount of Olives, where He went to pray so many times. On this agonizing occasion, Jesus wrestled with His Father and Himself. He knelt down and asked God to take the upcoming suffering away, but He also made it clear He wanted His Father's will to be done (v. 42). In verse 43 something wonderful happened. An angel from heaven appeared to strengthen Him. How loving of God the Father to send physical comfort in the form of an angel to help Jesus through this agony. Encouraged, He prayed so fervently that He sweat drops of blood. Jesus's internal struggle grew so great that He began to physically break. He so wanted to fulfill His Father's will, and at the same time, He did not want to go through the suffering ahead. But in the end, He was willing to move into the pain in order to accomplish God's purpose. He died to Himself with a willingness to endure the betrayal, the ridicule, the torture, and His ultimate death in order to provide life for those who accept Him.

Jesus took a moment during the Last Supper to talk individually and earnestly with Peter. Peter assured Him that he was prepared to go to prison and even die with Jesus (v. 33). But later that night, Peter three times denied knowing Him. As soon as Jesus's eyes met his, Peter realized what he had done. He had denied his master, the one to whom he had sworn allegiance, and he left weeping, a broken man.

While it's sometimes easy to have good intentions, it can be much more difficult to put those intentions into action. We can discuss and plan and be confident, but ultimately we must appropriate what we believe. Peter's intentions were excellent, but he wasn't able to follow through. Unable to handle the pressure of the moment, he denied his Savior three times. If Peter, one of Jesus's closest disciples, didn't have the strength to defend his Messiah, how will we? Let's take a moment to learn from Jesus Himself. We're reminded again that He regularly slipped away to spend time in prayer with His Father. He removed Himself from the people and spent time alone in fellowship with God. This gave Him the strength to face the most trying difficulties—from criticism by the religious leaders to torture and death by crucifixion. Only with His Father's help was He able to move forward.

We, too, can press into our difficult circumstances with God's help. Ephesians 6:18 says, "Praying at all times in the Spirit, with all prayer and supplication." Turning to Him, we can ask for His help to make it through tough times and live the life He has planned for us. Proverbs 2:6–8 says,

> For the LORD gives wisdom;
>   from his mouth come knowledge and understanding;
> he stores up sound wisdom for the upright;
>   he is a shield to those who walk in integrity,
> guarding the paths of justice
>   and watching over the way of his saints.

This is the way we as His followers survive, by looking to Him and receiving His supernatural and loving protection.

Finally, after a long night of turmoil that ended in His arrest, Jesus was brought before the high council to face charges. At this point, Jesus's time of mental and emotional unrest seemed to be over, and He accepted what He must do to save His people. It seems strange to consider such painful things just before Christmas when we normally celebrate love, joy, and peace. But unfortunately, some of us will also face difficulties that seem unbearable during the holiday season.

So how do we cope with these difficulties at Christmas or any other time? Do we have life events that we feel we can't handle? Certainly we aren't facing torture and death like Jesus, but we all have challenging circumstances and people that we must encounter. Maybe we have an unpleasant or even combative family member we will face over the holidays. While we hope for harmony during our gatherings, for many, the reality is conflict. Have we brought the problem to God and asked for His help? Or are we trying to solve things on our own? Perhaps it's time to wrestle with Him in prayerful meditation. If we earnestly seek Him, He will provide help in the form of the Holy Spirit to guide and fill our hearts and lives with His love and power. Romans 8:26 says, "The Spirit helps us in our weakness." We can't live a life filled with hope apart from Him. We need Him, and as our loving Father, He is always there waiting patiently for us.

Process

1. What causes fear in your life today?
2. Can you trust that God is always there for you? Do you believe that His Word is true?
3. Bring your problems to God and ask for His help. Worship Him, believing He will take care of you.

Prayer

Dear Lord, I turn to You, pleading for help to make it through tough times. This is the only way I can survive, by looking to You and receiving Your supernatural and loving protection from the enemy that wages war against my soul.

Promise

"For he has said, 'I will never leave you nor forsake you.'" (Hebrews 13:5)

Luke 23—Bow

*Now when the centurion saw what had taken place, he
praised God, saying, "Certainly this man was innocent!"*
—Luke 23:47

Do you like watching a movie more than once? My husband does.
In fact, to him, the more times he sees certain movies, the better they become! I'm not one of those people. Once I've watched
a movie, I'm done. But regardless, we enjoy watching movies
together. The big screen brings to life characters so relatable and
scenes so real that we feel we are right in the middle of the story.
Emotions rise and fall, and by the end of the movie, we're cheer-
ing for the good guy to win, the sick to be cured, the relationship
to be mended. Nothing upsets me more than to see credits roll
before a story comes to a satisfactory conclusion. I need to know
that all ends well and everything works out for the best.

In Luke 23, we are in the final days of Jesus's short life. These
last two chapters are like the end of an intense movie—only it was
real. Jesus had stirred up the people with His teachings and His
claim to be the Son of God, the Most High King (v. 5). The crowds
became outspoken and rowdy, including both those who believed
Jesus was the Son of God and those who did not. The disciples
continued asking questions about the future to which Jesus has
alluded.

The crowds grew larger and out of control. The religious leaders moved from agitation to anger and from disagreement to

disdain. Jesus's teachings had upended their ideology and religion. Their identity and worth had been drawn from an ancient stringent religious law, but Jesus spoke about abolishing this law. He explained that He had come to fulfill the law on their behalf, to exchange His perfect record for their unrighteousness. To them, this must have felt like a scandal, one that would take religious control from their hands. They must destroy this man who threatened the foundations upon which they had built their entire lives.

Jesus, the Son of God, the King of the Jews is the protagonist in Luke's story. He is the main character. The religious leaders as well as the governing authorities are the antagonists. They play the part of the villains, the ones who directly oppose Jesus. In an attempt to crucify Him emotionally, they mocked and ridiculed His claim to royalty when they dressed Jesus in a robe fit for a king (v. 11). They cried out, "If you are the King of the Jews, save yourself!" (v. 37). They hung a sign on the cross above His head that read "This is the King of the Jews" (v. 38). They placed a crown made of thorns on His head, further ridiculing His claim as king.

Hearing the people hurl verbal insults at His Son, God must have felt unimaginable pain as He looked on. The conflict of emotions surely was great. While God's heart was breaking for His only Son, He also knew that this was a necessary part of the plan to save the people. But He knew the end of the story. He wrote the ending. And *yes*, it ends just as we hope! God likely was thinking, *Just wait. You're about to find out that He really* is *the King.* But the mocking continued throughout the crucifixion until the moment of Jesus's last breath. The curtain closed but not without making its own statement. At the moment of Jesus's death, the temple's curtain ripped from top to bottom and the sun's light faded from the earth (vv. 45–46). The Roman centurion guarding the cross said, "Certainly this man was innocent!" (v. 47). Many of the people returned home beating their breasts, as if to say, "He really was the King!" And yes, still today, He reigns as our King of Kings and Lord of Lords.

Most of us know this story and its ending, so thankfully, it's as if we are watching this movie for a second time. We have a deep sense of relief knowing that although the enemy seemed to be winning the battle when Jesus was crucified, he lost the war when Jesus rose from the dead. Evil did not and will not win. God's plan did and will prevail. Paul reminded us:

> And let us run with endurance the race that is set before us, looking to Jesus, the founder and perfecter of our faith, who for the joy that was set before him endured the cross, despising the shame, and is seated at the right hand of the throne of God. Consider him who endured from sinners such hostility against himself, so that you may not grow weary or faint-hearted. (Hebrews 12:1–3)

Some of us may have the tendency to live our lives based on rules, much like the religious leaders in Jesus's day. But now, because of Jesus's death on our behalf, we can live a life of freedom based on His perfect record. This is grace. It is a gift we don't deserve and did nothing to merit. The birth we celebrate at Christmas offers unexplainable joy that comes with a new identity in our Savior. It's not because of anything we've done but because of everything Jesus did for us. If we accept Christ, we are named a child of the King, and we will receive all the benefits of true royalty! Riches untold belong to those who choose to believe that

Jesus is the Savior. We celebrate this good news not just at Christmas but every day of the year.

For all of eternity, the ultimate authority belongs to God. He is the final voice. His word is the first and last. The score will be evened, and the victory forever proclaimed! And for this we can be thankful, rejoice, and humbly bow at the feet of our loving and gracious King.

Process

1. What does faith mean in the face of adversity?
2. Write a prayer asking God to help you persevere hour by hour, day by day, trusting in Him as your loving Father.
3. How does a spirit of humility bring you peace?

Prayer

Holy Spirit, please remind me that if I earnestly seek You, You will provide help in my most challenging times. You will guide me and fill my heart and life with Your love and power. Please enable me to believe in Your presence and power.

Promise

"As I live, says the Lord, every knee shall bow to me,
  and every tongue shall confess to God." (Romans 14:11)

Luke 24—Triumph

He is not here, but has risen.

—Luke 24:6

It's not often we focus on the resurrection of Jesus on Christmas Eve. Traditionally, this is the day Christians celebrate His birth. But the hope that began with the baby in a manger is not complete without the message of His death and resurrection. So, which is more significant in the Christian faith: the celebration of Christmas and His birth or the celebration of Easter and His resurrection? The answer is both. His birth only makes sense when we also consider His resurrection. Today, we'll focus on the empty tomb as we behold the manger. On this holy Christmas Eve, let's celebrate Jesus's birth and resurrection by reflecting on the surprising parallel themes in both stories.

Parallel 1: The Spices. On Sunday morning, the third day after the crucifixion, several women including Mary, Mary Magdalene, and Joanna took spices to the tomb to anoint Jesus's body, lovingly caring for Him in His death. Similarly, at Jesus's birth, the wise men cared for Him by bringing gifts of gold, frankincense, and myrrh—spices used as perfumes and anointing oils.

Parallel 2: The Angels. Also on the glorious morning of the resurrection, the women found two angels at the empty tomb announcing that Jesus had risen from the dead (Luke 24:4–5). Similarly, a host of angels announced Jesus's birth to the shepherds, a heavenly host praising God and glorifying Him (Luke

2:13). Jubilant angels appeared in both stories, proclaiming the glory of God and the joy and excitement surrounding these wondrous events.

Parallel 3: The Cloths. When Peter ran to the empty tomb, he found only linen grave cloths in place of Jesus's body (24:12). Similarly, at Jesus's birth, his mother wrapped him in swaddling cloths to keep Him warm (2:7). These remind us of the humbling circumstances surrounding both the death and birth of Jesus. He had no place of burial until Joseph of Arimathea, a good and righteous member of the Jewish high council, laid Jesus's body in a new tomb. Likewise, born in a stable surrounded by animals, His life began in an unlikely and humble setting. This kingdom of God that Jesus brought to earth was not a kingdom of fame and riches and glory but rather of humility and relatable love.

Parallel 4: The Seekers. In both stories, we hear echoes of people searching for Jesus. Different groups came to the tomb looking for His body (24:2). They must have wanted to believe the hope that He brought to His people hadn't died along with Him. Similarly, at the time of Jesus's birth, the shepherds immediately began their search for the Messiah (2:15). In earnest anticipation, they could only imagine how the fulfillment of the prophecies would take place, from His birth all the way to His resurrection. In both stories, the people were searching for and reassured with hope.

Parallel 5: The News. After the crucifixion, word spread across the land that Jesus had risen from the dead (24:14). It probably spread as fast as the news of the long-awaited birth of the Savior (2:18). Bad news always travels fast, but good news sometimes travels almost as fast. Spreading the hope of Jesus was a privilege to all who believed, from the day He entered the world until the day He rose from the dead.

Parallel 6: The Prophecies. The message about the Savior's arrival and all that He would offer is mirrored in both stories through fulfillment of prophecy. After the resurrection, Jesus declared "that everything written about me in the Law of Moses and the Prophets and the Psalms must be fulfilled" (24:44). Similarly, circumstances surrounding Jesus's birth fulfilled the prophecies of the Old Testament (1:54–55). It was as if God knew those with less faith would need reassurance that the birth of a Savior and His death and resurrection were true!

Parallel 7: The Message of Love. The message of redeeming love found in both the Christmas and Easter stories offers comfort and joy to all who believe. His kindness and graciousness extend to a broken and sinful people. Longing for a Savior, many waited for and expressed deep desire for His message of hope. Soon after His birth, Anna the prophetess "began to give thanks to God and to speak of him to all who were waiting for the redemption of Jerusalem" (2:38). After the crucifixion, two men said, "But we had hoped that He was the one to redeem Israel" (24:21). Imagine how thrilling it must have been when they realized that this redemption had truly taken place!

Uniting imperfect people with a perfect God is unimaginable, but that is what Jesus did! Man is sinful; God is holy. Jesus paid for our sins when He hung from the cross. He is our forever sacrifice, reconciling all who choose to believe in Him as Savior and Lord. Jesus's life was given on our behalf as our sinful record was exchanged for His perfect one. From the bare, rustic wood of the manger to the crooked, distressed wood of the cross, God's perfect plan concerning His Son began before His birth and continued until after His death and throughout eternity. Luke 24 closes with Jesus speaking of such things: "The Christ should suffer and on the third day rise from the dead, and that repentance for the forgiveness of sins should be proclaimed in his name to all nations, beginning from Jerusalem" (vv. 46–47).

From the beginning of Jesus's life to the moment He rose from the dead, every promise He made came true. When we truly understand the beauty of the gospel and the freedom Jesus provides, we will worship and rejoice like never before. The triumph of life over death is the ultimate victory, and believing in Jesus results in a life of ultimate triumph. Now, may we move forward triumphantly through life as God shines His light on and through us and we are empowered and loved by Him. "Glory to God in the highest, and on earth peace among those with whom he is pleased" (2:14).

Process

1. How do you see yourself as an imperfect person connecting with a holy, perfect God?
2. Ask God to help you accept the kindness and graciousness offered through His Son, Jesus.
3. Write a statement to help you remember to live triumphantly based on your identity as a child of God.

Prayer

It's unimaginable that You, a perfect God, desire to be united with me, an imperfect human. Thank You for making this possible by sending Your Son, Jesus, to earth. He is the perfect imprint of Your character, God. He represents love and grace like I will never know here on earth.

Promise

"But thanks be to God, who gives us the victory through our Lord Jesus Christ." (1 Corinthians 15:57)

John 1—Shine

The true light, which gives light to everyone, was
coming into the world.

—John 1:9

In the twenty-four chapters of the book of Luke, we have seen a natural parallel to the twenty-four days in December leading to Christmas. But Luke doesn't have a chapter 25, so what about Christmas Day? What should we read? A logical ending might involve a chapter that summarizes everything we've learned about Jesus from Luke because Christmas Day represents the perfect happy ending. But does it? What if instead of the end, Christmas might actually represent the beginning?

Let's explore this idea by considering the meaning of the gospel in a personal way. Could a life lived in Jesus offer a continuous celebration of His birth and resurrection not only during this festive season but also every day? Since Jesus appeared on this earth as the Savior and conquered darkness by rising from the dead, we have the opportunity to live a new life in Him, our hearts forever changed. In fact, everything has changed, and we now have access to God through Jesus. So as we turn the page from the last chapter of Luke to the first chapter of John, we see a beautiful, compelling, and continued celebration beginning on Christmas Day!

In John 1, we receive a significant word from God. The message is love. The message is given to us from God. And the message is Jesus. What better way for God to communicate "I love you" than to send a message of compassion through His only Son? This is the clearest message mankind has ever received. It has lasted for more than two thousand years. No other message has had an impact on humanity like the love of God.

John tells us that the message of God's love through Jesus is the light of men (1:4). Just as in Luke 24 when we celebrated Jesus's birth and resurrection by looking at parallel themes, we celebrate in John 1 the theme of light, the essence of both Christmas and Easter. The story of Christmas began when Jesus was born on a dark night. This dark night transitioned into the bright light of the stars and the angels in the sky above. The next morning, the world awoke to a new dawn and, with it, the arrival of the promised Savior. Similarly, the story of the cross began with darkness covering the earth upon Jesus's death, followed by the utter darkness of the tomb. But that darkness transitioned into the morning light, which brought the discovery of a risen Savior. God's message of love to His people came in the form of His Son, a light that shone through the darkness of the world. This Messiah came to save us from our sin and offer us a new life with Him.

But while the message of both Christmas and Easter can forever impact us, we don't always feel its significance, live by its truth, or experience its resulting freedom. As life is woven with joys and hurts, victories and defeats, freedom and bondage, our experiences are filled with both belief and unbelief. This is why Jesus told the disciples, "This is the work of God, that you believe in him whom he has sent" (John 6:29). We see this message also in John 1:12: "But to all who did receive him, who believed in his name, he gave the right to become children of God." By the power of God's Spirit, we can truly believe that we are His beloved children. As a result, peace and hope abound rather than chaos and despair. We will have a radically different view of and experience in the world around us. Verse 16 says, "For from his fullness we have all received, grace upon grace."

We are beginning to see that this story doesn't have an ending, but instead, it is an ongoing narrative in which we have the privilege to play a part. Tomorrow, as you move into December 26, think back through the book of Luke. The message of truth is found in every chapter, as well as many other passages throughout the Bible. Relating to our loving Father every day will result in more joyful and purposeful lives.

So a merry and bright Christmas to you this glorious day on which we celebrate hope. Hope comes when light pierces the darkness and we are able to see clearly that our Savior has conquered death. Some of us might not feel the light of hope today. We might find ourselves fighting to experience truth and beauty, but in reality we are surrounded by hurt, pain, and difficulties. For us, Christmas is all about hope in Jesus rather than our unpredictable reality. Let's have faith in the hope that Christmas will be celebrated again, light will shine in darkness, and ultimately we will win because we are His. This truth, this light that shines in darkness, leads us to the King of all kings, who proclaimed a message of love and salvation by sending His Son to earth where death seemed to win on the cross but life won at the empty tomb. God promises that one day all wrongs will be made right (Revelation 21:4). Breathe. Rest. Rejoice. As you do, your life will shine like the bright star above the manger and the rising sun on resurrection day. May we never forget that the cross is what Christmas is all about! "In [Jesus] was life, and the life was the light of men. The light shines in the darkness, and the darkness has not overcome it" (vv. 4–5). God has made this known through Jesus.

HE IS RISEN. Today, tomorrow, and every day after that. This is the happiest of all endings and the most glorious beginning. Because of who He is, what He has done, and what He will continue to do, may we live in continuous anticipation and fulfillment of a beautiful life with Him. Every day.

Process

1. If you were to receive a personal message from God, what would you want it to say?

2. Jesus was born to shine a new light in this world. As you see Jesus shine on earth, how can you go and reflect His light on others?

3. Because of who Jesus is, what He has done, and what He will do, how can you live in continuous anticipation of a fulfilled life with Him? How can you remember that Christmas matters every day?

Prayer

By the power of Your Spirit, may I more truly believe that I am Your beloved child. Give me the gift of Your peace and hope rather than the chaos and despair I feel when I forget You are with me. This is the happiest of all endings and the most glorious beginning. Because of who You are, what You have done, and what You will continue to do, may I live in continuous anticipation and fulfillment of a beautiful life with You not only on Christmas Day but on every day.

Promise

"I am the light of the world. Whoever follows me will not walk in darkness, but will have the light of life." (John 8:12)

About the Authors

Anna Nash has a passion for helping people discover God's design for life and work. As a life coach, she focuses on finding their God-given purpose. Beacon People, a nonprofit organization, was birthed out of this calling. Other books by Anna include *path-Finder: A Journey Towards Purpose* and *wayMaker: A Journey Towards Seeing and Experiencing God Like Never Before*. She lives in Birmingham, Alabama, and is married to Tyler. They have four grown children and own Innova Coffee, a shop where she loves to share a fresh cup of coffee and warm conversation. Connect with Anna on her website annanash.net.

Katy Shelton graduated with a bachelor of science degree from Auburn University. She is a writer and editor who has been published on blogs, in magazines, and in newspapers. Katy is passionate about all things literary and especially enjoys the challenge of turning an idea into a powerful narrative. Born and raised in Birmingham, Alabama, she now lives south of the city on Lake Martin. Katy and her husband, John, have three sons—Jack, Drake, and Sullivan. *Christmas Matters* is her first book. Connect with Katy on her website at katyshelton.com.

Learn more about *Christmas Matters* at
annanash.net or katyshelton.com

If you enjoyed this book, will you consider sharing the message with others?

Let us know your thoughts. You can let the author know by visiting or sharing a photo of the cover on our social media pages or leaving a review at a retailer's site. All of it helps us get the message out!

Email: info@ironstreammedia.com

 @ironstreammedia

---

Iron Stream, Iron Stream Fiction, Iron Stream Kids, Brookstone Publishing Group, and Life Bible Study are imprints of Iron Stream Media, which derives its name from Proverbs 27:17, "As iron sharpens iron, so one person sharpens another." This sharpening describes the process of discipleship, one to another. With this in mind, Iron Stream Media provides a variety of solutions for churches, ministry leaders, and nonprofits ranging from in-depth Bible study curriculum and Christian book publishing to custom publishing and consultative services.

For more information on ISM and its imprints, please visit IronStreamMedia.com

ENJOY MORE FROM ANNA NASH AND KATY SHELTON AND DISCOVER THE POWER OF EASTER!

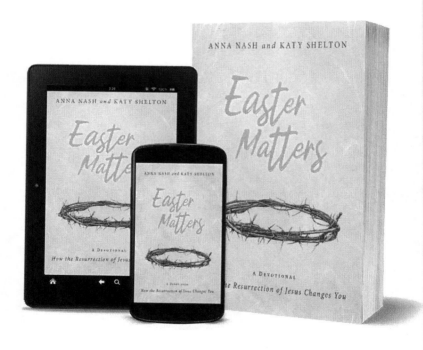

Available wherever books are sold.